Quick and Easy, Proven Recipes

Mediterranean Cooking

Publisher's Note: Raw or semi-cooked eggs should not be consumed by babies, toddlers, pregnant or breastfeeding women, the elderly or those suffering from a chronic illness.

Publisher & Creative Director: Nick Wells
Senior Project Editor: Catherine Taylor
Art Director: Mike Spender
Layout Design: Jane Ashley
Digital Design & Production: Chris Herbert

Special thanks to Ann Nicol, Esme Chapman and Frances Bodiam.

This is a **FLAME TREE** Book

FLAME TREE PUBLISHING
Crabtree Hall, Crabtree Lane
Fulham, London SW6 6TY
United Kingdom
www.flametreepublishing.com

First published 2014

ISBN: 978-1-78361-245-1

Printed in Singapore
All images are courtesy of Flame Tree Publishing Limited except the following which are courtesy of **Shutterstock.com** and © the following contributors: 13 Mircea BEZERGHEANU; 4 Nolte Lourens; 6 Catherine Jones; 7 Josef Bosak; 8 Alan Kraft; 9, 58–59 Phillip Lange; 10 tomy; 11 Gueorgui Ianakiev; 12, 79 Eve's Food Photography; 16 Vladimir Melnik ; 17 Melisa Mok Mun Chee; 18 Mandy Godbehear; 19 Jean Morrison; 20 Matt Trommer; 21 Marek Slusarczyk; 22 Steve Beer; 23 bouzou; 24–25 Anobis; 26 Victoria Goncharenko; 27 Volfoni; 28 cyrrpit; 29 Elena Elisseeva; 30 ultimathule; 31 inacio pires; 32 Patrycja Zadros; 33 francesco riccardo iacomino; 34 Dino; 35 Yanta; 36, 147 Paul Cowan; 37 Ray Hub; 38–39 Andrey Grinyov; 40 Jan Martin Will; 41 Christian Musat; 42 Emily Goodwin; 43 BlueOrange Studio; 44 Tania Zbrodko; 45 vospalej; 46 kucedra; 47 Tomo Jesenicnik; 48 Mr. Kyryl Rudenko; 49 EVRON; 50 asliuzunoglu; 51 Maria Bell; 52 Styve Reineck; 53, 61 Holger Mette; 54 diak; 55 Ramzi Hachicho; 56 Arkady Mazor; 57 Evgeni Gitlits; 60; Holger Mette; 62, 66 WitR; 63 Christophe Robard; 64 Kit Oates; 65 JIS; Stana; 67 Anthony Maragou; 68 Dhoxax; 69 Boris Stroujko; 85 Josep M Penalver Rufas; 95 Liv friis-larsen; 103 Piccia Neri; 109 nito; 113 jabiru; 119, 127, 171, 237 Patty Orly; 141 Martin Turzak; 149 travellight; 159 Olaf Speier; 205 Lilyana Vynogradova; 239 bernashafo; 245 Ana del Castillo.

Quick and Easy, Proven Recipes

Mediterranean Cooking

**FLAME TREE
PUBLISHING**

Contents

Introduction

The sparkling, crystal-clear waters of the Mediterranean Sea connect a number of countries that may not always spring to mind as being 'Mediterranean'. But each of the countries covered in this book has a Mediterranean coastline and often a climate to match, so that their cuisine embodies many of the classic elements of Mediterranean cooking. In this exciting book we travel around the Mediterranean, from Spain, France and Italy in the west through to North Africa and Asia, via Greece, Crete and Cyprus in the east. We will discover the common characteristics and the traditions of food in the different countries. But we will also become aware that each of the countries has been influenced over the years by other Mediterranean countries, in addition to the climate and the choice of livestock and vegetables.

Health Benefits

People often refer to the 'Mediterranean diet', claiming that it is one of the healthiest diets in the world. However there is no one Mediterranean diet, as there are enormous differences in culture, ethnic background, religion, agricultural production and taste. Common threads that we will see in most of these Mediterranean diets and dishes is the relative high consumption of fruit, vegetables, potatoes, cereals, beans, nuts and seeds, as well as salads. With some notable exceptions dairy products are a lot less important than fish and poultry and, comparatively to Europe or North America for example, very little red meat

is eaten. Eggs are not consumed in the quantities seen in many other countries and, for many of these societies bordering the Mediterranean, where the grape is grown to create wine, the consumption levels of alcohol are surprisingly low.

More than half of the fat calories in a Mediterranean diet come from monounsaturated fats, which do not raise blood cholesterol levels in the same way that saturated fat does. This is one of the key reasons why the Mediterranean diet is considered to be so healthy. Olive oil, beloved of most Mediterranean cooking, is a vital source of monounsaturated fat. This means that the occurrence of heart disease in Mediterranean countries is lower than in the rest of Europe or North America. Coupled with this is the lifestyle, with the tendency towards more physical activity and extended families.

The commonly grown olive is claimed to have remarkable properties; not only does it provide monounsaturated fat, but it is also beneficial to the digestive system. Many claim that it not only helps to eliminate stomach ulcers but can also deal with internal infections and problems with the gall bladder. With so many major olive oil-producing countries around the Mediterranean Sea there is always stiff competition and lively debate as to which country produces the finest olive oil. In the west there are the vast olive groves of Spain and southern France, at the heart of the Mediterranean the Italian crop is grown and to the east each and every Greek island and parts of the mainland, together with vast, ancient plantations in Asia Minor, provide large quantities of the precious oil.

Following a strict Mediterranean diet has even been shown to provide protection against heart disease, cancer,

Parkinson's disease and Alzheimer's. Effectively it is a lighter way of eating. Much of the meat is grilled rather than fried or it is slow cooked in an oven. Desserts often include home grown fruits and honey is used to sweeten dishes rather than refined sugar.

Culture

Food is an integral part of family life and culture across the whole of the Mediterranean. It is at the heart of people's hospitality. The flavours are robust, clear and uncomplicated and make full use of the gentle climate and the fertile soil. Onions, garlic, tomatoes and olive oil are at the heart of many of the dishes. Whilst Egyptians may prefer fava beans, the French favour green beans and the Tuscans cannellini beans. Yet these form the basis of very similar dishes. Proximity to the sea means that fish and shellfish feature in soups, stews and pastas. Smaller animals, such as sheep, goats and rabbit provide the majority of the meat. It is from sheep and goats that a great deal of the cheeses and yogurts are made.

Many people still cook in the traditional way, or using modern variations of open flames and simple ovens. Across the regions there are squashes, peppers, cucumbers, artichokes, okra, lettuces and a profusion of fresh herbs from rosemary and basil to fennel, mint and oregano.

Identity

The various Mediterranean countries share far more than one virtually landlocked sea and an enormous beach around that ocean. They share a common heritage, a common perspective on life and food. They place their vegetables, fruits and livestock at the heart of their lives and their diets.

For generations they have relied on the sea and the soil to provide them with timely, seasonal bounties of nutritious, largely organic and delicious food and drinks.

Many of the traditional recipes have been passed down from generation to generation, mother to daughter, over the centuries. Yet from family to family, village to village and country to country these basic recipes have taken on separate identities, reflecting the culture and traditions of the people and the regions.

No two Italian cooks, French chefs or Greek taverna owners will agree with even the essential ingredients of a common sauce or simple vegetable dish. The dishes have evolved with experimentation and the use of regional or seasonal variations.

Mediterranean food is a feast for meat lovers, seafood devotees and for vegetarians. There is something in the diet for everyone and for any occasion. For Mediterranean people food is something to be shared and lingered over. They are fiercely proud of their culinary heritage, whether it has a distinctly French, Greek, Italian, Spanish or Moroccan influence.

Mediterranean Cooking gives you a taste of the dishes that are served in luxurious villas on the French Riviera, in the hills of Tuscany, on the mosaic of Greek islands or in exotic Marrakesh. The recipes incorporate the basics of style and technique, but also show you the more sophisticated Mediterranean recipes; it is a cookbook that entertains as well as educates.

Landscapes and Culture

From the sun-kissed beaches of southern Spain through the lush mountainous regions of Greece to the pyramids of Egypt, the landscape and culture of the Mediterranean is as beautiful as it is varied. Taking each region in turn, this chapter introduces the diverse cuisine and local specialities of the countries bordering the Mediterranean sea. From bouillabaisse in Provence to falafel in Syria, take a leap into the mouth-watering world of Mediterranean cooking.

Spain

Surrounded by water and situated at the crossroads of the Mediterranean Sea and the Atlantic Ocean, Spain has an ancient maritime tradition, which is reflected in its cuisine. Influenced by fresh seafood and healthy, home-grown produce, the country's history, culture and different regions all contribute to its varied array of dishes. It has a predominantly dry and mountainous terrain, although its varied landscape ranges from lush countryside to rugged coastlines. The mountainous areas are perfect terrain for the rearing of goats and sheep, both of which are used in many Spanish recipes.

The tradition of growing wheat flourished during Roman times. Its quality was so good that the trend for using the grain had already spread throughout Spain, Greece and parts of North Africa. Onions and garlic were introduced to the Spaniards by the Phoenicians and tomatoes, potatoes and peppers from South America or the Caribbean. The Romans heavily influenced Spanish cuisine, as did the Moors, who left behind the use of honey and cumin in Spanish dishes, particularly those dishes that are still cooked in the southern regions of the country today. The Moors also introduced the use of almonds and egg yolks in the making of Spanish desserts.

There are several recipes that are common to the various regions of Spain, including Tortilla de Patata (potato omelette), paella, stews, such as Pork Stew with Saffron Rice, and recipes based on pulses, such as chickpeas and lentils, as the major ingredient. But the regional variations in recipes make Spain's cuisine even more diverse. Madrid is famous for

Cocido Madrileño (chickpea stew) and Callos a la Madrilène (made from tripe). Catalonia has a long tradition of being famous for its rice dishes and the quality of its seafood. Despite this, perhaps the best-known Catalonian dish is Crema Catalana, very much like a crème brûlée. Other favourite Spanish desserts include flans, and cakes such as Madeleines, as well as custard, rice pudding, torrijas and churros. Torrijas are slices of bread soaked in milk and sugar (or sometimes wine), coated in egg, fried in oil and drizzled with syrup or honey, or sprinkled with sugar and cinnamon. Churros are similar to doughnuts and named for their shape, which is said to resemble the horns of the sheep bred in Castile. Churros can be thick or thin and are usually dipped in coffee or hot chocolate at breakfast time.

The region of La Rioja, as well producing its well-known wine, is renowned for its vegetable soups and its pepper and potato dishes, while in the west of Spain the area of Extremadura is famous for Cocido Extremeño, a rich stew made from bacon, poultry, ham and vegetables. Andalucia has a long tradition of fish and seafood, especially shrimps, squid, mackerel and flat fish, and Murcia is known for fish and lamb stews. Valencia, the home of Spain's famous paella, still celebrates public holidays by cooking huge dishes of paella in the streets, making them as colourful and tempting as possible. Paella is popular throughout Spain, including the islands, and traditionally families enjoy the dish at Sunday lunchtime.

The central region of Spain is unsurprisingly less influenced by the sea and is well known for roast meats, such as lamb, veal, and young pigs and goats. The meat is roasted slowly in a wood-fired oven until it is extremely tender and full of flavour.

The Balearic Islands of Mallorca, Menorca, Ibiza and Formentera have a typical Catalonian tradition of seafood dishes, together with simple dishes predominantly

comprising vegetables. Tumbet, a dish of fried potatoes, peppers and aubergine in a tomato stew similar to France's ratatouille is a prime example, although Majorca in particular is renowned for its pastries, called Ensaimadas, which are warm, yeast-based cakes that are made into round, coiled shapes. They are sliced into individual portions and served with hot coffee or drinking chocolate, much like Churros.

The famous Spanish tradition of a tapas bar can be found in even the smallest of Spanish villages. The word tapa means 'lid' (from tapar, 'to cover'), so the use of this word to mean 'snack' is believed to have originated from the plate of appetizers that hosts would place over their guests' glasses to prevent flies entering the glasses. There is no absolute recipe for tapas; they can include cheeses, fish, eggs, vegetables, dips and pastries or can simply be a slice of toasted bread dipped in olive oil and garlic, a dish of olives, slices of ham or salami, pieces of Spanish tortilla or marinated anchovies. Meatballs in tomato sauce, garlic mushrooms, shrimp or cooked chorizo in wine are all offered in tapas bars around Spain. Tapas are displayed on or in the bar for guests to choose.

Certainly olive oil is an indispensable ingredient of many Spanish recipes, as is garlic, which is added to most dishes. Spanish cooking uses a variety of meat in large quantities, depending on farming and tradition in the region. Chicken, pork and rabbit feature frequently, as do sausages and salamis, particularly chorizo, which is a spicy and very popular Spanish sausage. Also popular are prawns, shrimps, anchovies and sardines.

Gazpacho is a famous Spanish soup, made from a mixture of tomato, olive oil, garlic, cucumbers and croutons, and is served chilled. As for drinks, sangria is a red wine and fruit punch that can be found everywhere in Spain and Rioja (from La Rioja in northern Spain) is one of Spain's leading varieties of wine, together with Valdepeñas and a number of Cavas, which are sparkling wines. Jerez, or Spanish sherry, is regularly consumed in Spanish bars, restaurants and homes.

France

France's reputation for haute cuisine has evolved over the centuries, but there still remains a diverse regional recipe variation. The French have a refined style of cooking, which is the result of both political and social changes throughout the centuries. Some of their national dishes and recipes originated as regional ones, particularly their breads and cheeses, but the fall of the monarchy during the French Revolution put many chefs out of work and they were forced to sell food to the general public through their newly established restaurants, rather than cook for the rich and famous.

Until this time the diet of the French peasant had consisted mainly of what they could grow themselves. But by 1914 and the First World War, with improved distribution and transportation throughout France, different foods and cattle were introduced to the recipes of the general public. Three main chefs are credited with refining French cuisine over the centuries, namely François Pierre de la Varenne (1618–78), Marie-Antoine Carême (1784–1833) and Georges Auguste Escoffier (1846–1935), the latter being possibly the most influential of the three. Escoffier introduced lighter sauces and reduced the number of spices used in the recipes, as well as laying down set procedures for subsequent cooks to follow.

When referring to Mediterranean cuisine and France, you can only really mean the southern half of France, more particularly the coastal regions. Southern France is colloquially known as Le Midi ('noon' in French, derived from the old French for 'middle' and 'day'), as the sun is always in the south at noon in France (and the rest of the Northern Hemisphere). One

significant part of southern France is the Languedoc-Roussillon region (pictured page 28, left), which is particularly famed for its vineyards around Bordeaux, although it also produces abundant cheeses, olive oils and pies known as Petits Pâtés de Pezenas. But the really Mediterranean feel starts when you reach Provence, the Riviera and the French island of Corsica...

In these areas, olive trees are grown in abundance; the warmer climate and proximity of these regions to the Mediterranean Sea make the production of olive oil a successful industry here. Provence olive oil is of the highest quality and enhances many traditional Provençal recipes, used instead of the butters and creams used in many other parts of France. Provence also boasts an abundance of fresh fruit and vegetables, which are complemented by the wide range of herbs, many of which can be found growing wild throughout the region. Honey is the natural sweetener for many Provence recipes, made by the bees from the Provençal wild flowers and the carpets of lavender for which the region is famous. Fish from the Mediterranean Sea are simply grilled, as is the locally reared meat, which has thrived from eating the wild rosemary growing throughout the area.

Provençal specialities range from simple salads to stuffed vegetables, grilled lamb chops served with herbs de Provence and the famous fish dish bouillabaisse. This dish is made with at least three kinds of fresh fish cooked in a broth with onions, tomatoes, saffron and various herbs, such as laurel, sage and thyme. The soup is served with toast and rouille, a spicy sauce that some mix into the broth and others choose to spread onto the toast. The most renowned bouillabaisse dish is cooked in the city of Marseille. Other Provençal dishes have been influenced by the region's geography; in the north the mountain cuisine is based on cheese and cured meats, whilst in the south the Mediterranean Sea provides its bounty of fish.

The cuisine of the sunny Côte d'Azur or French Riviera uses olive oil, citrus fruits and aromatic herbs in many dishes, but also incorporates produce from the inner regions of France, such as young kid, strong cheeses and fresh vegetables. This region's dishes tend to be a blend of French and Italian cuisine, using a mix of olive oil and butter, with the influences of several Mediterranean countries appearing in the dishes from time to time.

Salade Niçoise is a speciality of the Côte D'Azur, originating in and named after the city of Nice and made popular during the 1880s. Served on a flat plate, ripe tomato wedges, halved boiled new potatoes, steamed green beans and wedges of hard-boiled eggs are arranged on a bed of crisp lettuce and topped with tinned tuna in olive oil and Niçoise olives. The salad is garnished with tinned anchovies and served with traditional Dijon vinaigrette.

A world away from mainland France, goats and sheep inhabit the island of Corsica in abundance, so it is not surprising that the meat from kids and lambs are used in traditional Corsican dishes, such as the meat stew known as stufato, and ragout, which is a meat stew that can also be added to pasta dishes. The Corsicans also enjoy simple, roasted meat dishes. The island's high-quality home-reared pork is used to make hams, dried pork fillet, dried sausage, Pancetta, bacon and smoked and dried liverwurst. Chestnuts are grown in the Corsican Castagniccia forest and are often used to produce flour for making bread, cakes and polenta. Acorns from the Castagniccia forest are also used as animal food for the island's pigs and boars.

Fresh fish and seafood dishes are served regularly, as are the locally grown clementines, lemons, nectarines and figs. Candied citrus fruit is used in cake recipes and to make nougat, and the island's brocciu cheese, made from sheep's or goats' milk, together with the chestnuts, are used in Corsica's dessert recipes.

€
5,00 Kilo Ail
Vrac

produit		catégorie I
variété	Ail Blanc	
calibre		

1kg

Italy

e

T he 'boot' of Italy, along with its islands of Sicily and Sardinia, sits proudly in the centre of the Mediterranean Sea and, with its roots dating back to before Christ, modern-day Italian cuisine is one of the most popular in the Mediterranean, and in fact the world.

There are distinctions between the recipes of the north and south of Italy, as well as between deep inland and the coastal regions and islands, mainly because of Italy's history of European cultures – from the Etruscans and the Romans to the Renaissance and the Baroque. It was the discovery of the New World that brought about the introduction of potatoes, tomatoes, bell peppers and maize to Italy and it was during the Middle Ages that food preservation, by smoking or bottling in brine, became an important role for any cook. Because the Mediterranean trade routes were strongly controlled by the Arab countries, the southern regions of Italy were heavily influenced by this in their choice of recipes. But the Roman and Germanic cultures strongly affected the northern regions. Certainly over the years the development of regional Italian recipes and cuisine has progressed. Each region has its own specialities, which has stemmed from bordering countries like France and Austria, or the closeness to the Mediterranean Sea or the mountains. Italian cuisine is seasonal and boasts the use of fresh, locally grown produce.

The recipes of Italy's northeastern region of Fruili-Venezia Giulia are influenced by Austria, Hungary, Slovenia and

Croatia with sausages, goulash, sauerkraut, dumplings, strudels and polenta, used as an accompaniment to meat, fish and cheese dishes. With Venice as its capital city, the region of Veneto is famous for risotto, made from seafood on the coast, or from pumpkin, asparagus, radish or frogs' legs inland, as well as dishes of pasta and borlotti or cannellini beans, such as Pasta Fagioli. Risotto is also popular in Lombardy, as are rice soups and regional cheeses like Gorgonzola, but heartier soups and roasted and braised meats are customary in the Val D'Aosta region.

Surrounded on three sides by the Alps and with Turin as its capital, the region of Piedmont relies on the changing seasons for its recipes. Fish, nuts, garlic, truffles, vegetables and fungi are all used regularly and the cheese Castelmagno is produced. Piedmont's preferred preserved dish is Filetto Baciato, which involves a white-wine-marinated pork fillet being coated with salami paste and cured for at least six months.

The north-Italian region of Emilia-Romagna is reputedly the pasta capital, laying claim to many of its own pasta types and dishes, including Bologna's famed tagliatelle and meat sauce. However, polenta was in fact the former staple at least of many mountainous areas of this region, particularly in the Apennine Mountain towns and villages. There is also a tradition for producing balsamic vinegar, Parmesan cheese, Parma, pancetta and other cured hams.

Tuscany and Umbria boast many simple, home-grown foods. Mushrooms, vegetables, fruit, olives, herbs, truffles and freshly caught fish are popular and in the coastal area of Marche, in addition to fish and seafood, sausages and home-cured ham are produced. Neighbouring Lazio's cuisine is heartier and shows signs of a Jewish influence in its use of artichokes and spicy and hearty pasta dishes, whilst to the east, the people of Abruzzo prefer hot and spicy lamb and pasta dishes, flavoured with their locally grown chillies. The Abruzzo area is renowned for its production of saffron, which is used in many Italian dishes.

In Campania (Capri and Prócida islands, in the Gulf of Naples, are pictured opposite and on page 33 respectively), durum wheat is used to make pasta, and sauces and pizzas are often topped with the region's mozzarella cheese, made from water buffalo milk. Dried durum wheat pasta is also an important export of the Apulia (Puglia) region, also in the south, where olive oil production is the highest in the country. The people of neighbouring Basilicata prefer to have meat as the accompaniment to their durum wheat pasta, particularly pork.

In the 'toe' of Italy, Calabria has a varied cultural past and this is reflected in its people's favourite recipes – the Arabs introduced citrus fruits, raisins, artichokes and aubergines, for instance, and cookery skills were influenced during the House of Anjou and Napoleon Bonaparte eras and by the Spanish. Much seafood and fresh fish is eaten in this region and melons and watermelons are grown as a local speciality.

The islands of Sicily and Sardinia (Sardinia is pictured on page 30) have their own speciality dishes. Sicilian cuisine was influenced by the Ancient Greeks (wine), the Romans (goose) and the Byzantines, who introduced many new flavours to the island. During the tenth and eleventh centuries the Arabs introduced more new flavours, with apricots, sugar, citrus fruits, melons, rice, raisins and spices, such as nutmeg, clove and cinnamon. Later, in 1194, the Hohenstaufens became the Germanic Kings of Sicily and influenced the diet with the introduction of meats, and then the Spanish became the main influence by introducing cocoa, maize, tomatoes and turkey. Being islands, Sicilians and Sardinians enjoy seafood and fish, such as rock lobster, scampi, squid, tuna, sardines, cuttlefish and swordfish.

As with many Mediterranean countries, the Italians enjoy appetizers, such as antipasti washed down with a good wine. These snack-size portions are often also eaten between meals or to accompany drinks for guests, as it is considered impolite or unhealthy to serve alcohol without food. Like the varying specialities and cuisines throughout Italy, there is also a wide variety of wine-producing regions, totalling around 20 throughout the country, producing the largest amount of wine in the world and regulated very closely by the Italian government.

Greece ❧ Cyprus

reek food has evolved over the centuries, influenced by the numerous invasions the country has suffered at the hands of the Minoans, the Romans, the Byzantines, the Italians, the Arabs and the Turks.

But there are still some dishes that can be traced back to the Ancient Greeks, involving ingredients such as nuts, garlic, olive oil, lemons, sesame, honey, cheeses and dried meats. Natural ingredients which are grown locally, freshly picked and cooked on the same day are all important elements of Greek cuisine.

Scattered around the eastern Mediterranean, Greece's islands are sun-kissed with a temperate climate. This provides the country with an abundance of fresh vegetables, fruits and herbs to use in their excellent cuisine. In addition, most of Greece is less than 130 km (80 miles) from the Mediterranean Sea, so fish plays an important role in its cuisine too. Kalamari, or squid, is served as a starter or a main course and this can be griddled with lemon or fried in batter. Fish roe dip, or taramasalata, can form part of a Greek mezethes (a selection of snacks rather like tapas), along with tzatziki (cucumber and yogurt dip) or aubergine dip.

The lushness of the slopes of the many mountainous regions throughout Greece enable the sheep and goats living on them to thrive. The Greeks eat the meat and use

the milk of these animals to make feta cheese, which is used in their salads, along with olives, which grow in abundance in the country, most famously on the island of Crete. Cheese and spinach pies, or simply cheese pies, are made from feta or other local cheeses, using filo pastry and offered to guests or eaten as a starter or main dish accompanied by a salad.

Because Greece comprises such a large number of smaller islands in addition to its mainland, the country's recipes are extremely diverse – each of the islands has its own way of selecting and preparing the ingredients. Many of the islands also have their own specialities, normally based around their success at growing one of the ingredients locally. Greek cooking is very frugal; and the Greeks tend to cook whatever they have available in the garden, so dishes are seasonal, and when fresh food is not available they turn to dried foods. Little use is made of a freezer in Greece.

Lamb plays an important role in Greek food and is often served as a celebration dish. It is spit roasted, slow roasted in the oven, stewed or casseroled. Minced lamb is used in moussaka, together with sliced aubergine, garlic, onion and béchamel sauce topped with grated cheese. Minced lamb can also be added to the small, new leaves of the grapevine, along with rice and herbs, to make dolmades, or stuffed vine leaves.

Crete is the largest of the Greek islands. It sits in the centre of the eastern Mediterranean basin, where the continents of Europe, Asia and Africa meet. Crete has one of the oldest cuisine traditions in the world; tastes, smells, ingredients and skills have all survived from prehistoric times. Their diet is rich in vegetables, pulses, fruits, cereals, salads, fish and grilled meat and their major source of fat is olive oil: very little butter is used for cooking. They season their food with herbs and make their sesame-topped bread with yeast. They also eat mountain snails, which can be cooked in a number of different ways.

The value of honey has been appreciated in Crete since ancient times. In the Egyptian Papyruses, honey is mentioned as a healing treatment and the ancient Indians claimed that drinking honey and milk daily would preserve and prolong life. In Greek mythology Zeus was raised on honey from the nymph bee and both Hippocrates and Aristotle recommended honey for the healing of many illnesses. The Egyptians offered honeycombs to their gods as a precious gift of loyalty and consolation.

Greek recipes in general have been strongly influenced by Turkish and Middle Eastern cuisine and as an independent island Crete is self-sufficient in year-round fresh fruit and vegetables, as well as in seafood. Cretan specialities are the local Graviera cheese (much like Gruyère) and Myzithra, a creamy white cheese that is often served instead of feta cheese in Greek salads.

Determined by the seasons, dishes are cooked with what is available. By October the grapes have been picked and dried, so sweet recipes involve sultanas and the wholesome sweet dish called mustalevriá, which is made from the leftovers of the grape pressing and winemaking. In November the walnuts are ready and dishes are made combining these with honey and yogurt. Then the oranges are ready by January and many Cretan housewives preserve them to make gliká tou koutalioú, which literally transcribes to 'sweet of the spoon', a process much like jam-making. The sugar preserves the fruit, which can also be figs, apricots, cherries, quince and grapes and these treats are kept in the store cupboard to offer to guests with their coffee.

Another Cretan staple is a dried, rusk-like bread that is traditionally made throughout Greece with barley or whole meal. It is sliced three quarters of the way through before being baked. These dákos can be broken into chunks and added to a Greek salad, or they can be used to make a well-known Greek dish also called dákos. The rusks are drizzled

with water and olive oil to soften them and tomatoes are grated on top of the dried slices. Salt, pepper, olive oil and feta cheese are used to top the dákos, together with green or black olives.

Cyprus (pictured left), a former British colony, is the third largest island in the Mediterranean Sea. In 1974 it was invaded by the Turks, who successfully occupied a third of the island's land, in the north. Cuisine in the non-Turkish southern areas of Cyprus is traditionally Greek, but with the expected island-specific slant. Halloumi cheese is a speciality of Cyprus and is made from a mixture of goat's and sheep's milk with mint leaves. Usually grilled as an appetizer, sometimes with Lountza, a Cypriot ham, the method for making this cheese originated in Cyprus. Other traditional Cypriot dishes centre around the fresh produce and the fruit of the sea. Squid, octopus, sea bass and red mullet are all used regularly in dishes, as are salads and vegetables, which are also pickled to preserve them.

Cypriot meat specialities include sheftalia, which is minced meat that has been moulded into a sausage-shape and wrapped in the intestines of the animal. Most Cypriot meat is marinated before cooking, often in olive oil, wine, lemon juice and dried coriander. Bulgur wheat is used regularly in Cypriot recipes, as are nuts, artichokes and fresh figs.

Throughout Greece and Cyprus the small, hot or cold, fish, vegetable, meat or fruit dishes make up the mezethes or meze. Originally served by housewives to their guests, these meze were literally whatever was left in the kitchen. The small dishes are served with drinks, whether it is wine (Krasomezethes) or a glass of the fiery Greek Ouzo (Ouzomezethes). Greek eating is all about company. Because of the temperate climate the Greeks tend to eat late at night and to entertain guests often and it never matters if unexpected guests arrive; the Greek housewife can always compile an ad hoc meze to offer them.

Albania

Situated between Greece, Macedonia, Kosovo and Montenegro, like most of the countries that border the Mediterranean, Albania's cuisine has been influenced over the years by the occupation of other countries. Greece, Italy and the Ottoman Turks all occupied Albania and each has left its mark on their cuisine; over the years Albania has accumulated styles from the Balkan as well as Mediterranean nations. Before this, Albania's different regions had their own unique styles of cooking, but Communist rule obliterated these separate identities and now their recipes are countrywide.

Albania's vegetation is rich and their recipes combine ingredients with spices, oregano, olives and grapes. Seafood specialities are common in the coastal areas of Durrës, Vlorë and Sarandë. Albania's mild climate favours agriculture so they grow and cook peppers, aubergines, tomatoes, cucumbers and vegetables. These are used with meats and fish to form dishes often baked in earthenware pots or sautéed to make stews, casseroles, stuffed vegetables or meatballs.

Olives are a staple and are grown in Berat, Vlora, Borsh, Himara and Tirana. Frequently these are eaten alone, or as part of a meze, but are often combined with meats and vegetables as an essential ingredient in traditional Albanian dishes. Albanians also use a variety of spices to enhance the flavour; garlic and hot peppers are popular, as are lemons, vinegar and yogurt, although these are added by taste rather than following recipes. Many Albanians make and consume yogurt daily, together with buttermilk; these two ingredients are used countrywide as the basis for sauces and other dishes.

Albanian cheeses still tend to vary by region, with the most popular countrywide a white cheese made from sheep's milk. This originated in the south of Albania and is similar to Greek feta cheese and similarly added to home-grown salads.

The South Slavic Countries

Slovenia, Croatia, Bosnia and Herzegovina and Montenegro all border the Mediterranean Sea. Unsurprisingly, it is the coastal areas of these countries that are more typically 'Mediterranean' food-wise. With a varied terrain and climate, Slovenian cuisine varies from region to region. Many base their dishes on bacon, lard, dripping, mushrooms, pork, flour-based dishes, potatoes, beans, butter, cream and eggs. Others include porridge, stew and one-pot meals, like soups from turnip peel or beef and chicken soups, served on special occasions. Kettle goulash (*bogracs gulyas*) is a one-pot beef dish that includes bacon fat, paprika, sour cream and seasoning. The dishes from Bela Krajina and Primorska are based around mutton and goat's meat or poultry, whilst in Dolenjska and Notranjska they eat roasted dormouse, quail and hedgehog.

The inner regions of Croatia have been influenced over the years by the Turks, Hungarians and Viennese; and the Mediterranean regions by the Greeks, Romans, Italians and French. The sea provides the coastal regions with squid, cuttlefish, tuna, shrimps, mussels, cod, clams and lobster, whilst other regions specialize in soups, stews, pasta, spicy garlic sausages, sheep's and goat's cheese and salty pies, like Dalmatian vegetable pie. The Viennese-influence shows in the pastries and cakes.

The food of Bosnia (pictured right) is influenced by the Turkish, Greeks and Central Europe. They use moderate spices, cook their food in plenty of water and fresh vegetables are used regularly. Pilaf and goulash are popular meals and dessert recipes originate from Greece and Turkey.

The food of Montenegro (pictured left) is distinctively Italian, particularly its bread-making style, meat curing and drying, cheese making, soups and stews, polenta, stuffed capsicums and love of meatballs. However they also serve moussaka, pitta, kebab and Hungarian goulash, whilst for dessert they enjoy baklava and crepes.

Turkey

Although the Mediterranean regions of Turkey use fresh fruit, vegetables and fish, the other regions definitely have their own style of cuisine. Heavily influenced by the Ottoman Dynasty for six centuries, and by western countries in more recent years, Turkish cuisine has become world famous. The temperate climate and the country's long history of farming and cooking make it unsurprising that Turkish food has become a popular option in most European countries. Turkey is known for a diversity of dishes because of its rich flora, fauna and regional differentiation.

Like most Mediterranean countries Turkey still has some regional specialities. The north is famous for corn and anchovies, the southeast for dishes similar to those in Greece, like the sweet pastries baklava and kadayif, as well as kebabs, and central Anatolia shows an Italian influence in its love of pasta dishes. This diverse and traditional cuisine is an integral aspect of Turkish culture. It is a part of their rituals and of everyday life, reflecting spirituality through symbolism and practice.

Bread dough, or ekmek, is one Turkish speciality, which originated with the Ottomans, that forms the basis of many of their traditional meals. The dough is used to make many varieties of bread and also dumplings, one of which is Manti. These dumplings are filled with meat mix and eaten with garlic yogurt, melted butter and paprika.

Kebabs are another favourite throughout the country, originating with the nomadic Turks, who grilled their meat over camp fires. Shish kebab is grilled cubes of skewered meat, whilst doner kebabs are made from stacked alternating layers of minced meat and sliced leg of lamb. These are rotated on a large upright skewer, in front of a vertical grill and, as they cook, thin slices are shaved and served.

Syria

ℰ

The Syrian Arabic Republic lies on the eastern coast of the Mediterranean Sea, with Lebanon, Israel, Jordan, Iraq and Turkey as its border countries. With agriculture a primary industry for thousands of years, fresh produce has always been an important aspect of Syrian food. Despite numerous conquests from the Greeks, the Romans and the Persians, the Arabic culture has been maintained in Syria to a large extent, however many Syrian dishes have also been strongly influenced by the Greeks, the Asians, the Turkish and the French, mainly because of Syria's important position on the former east-west Silk Road or trade route.

Syrian recipes include many dishes that use rice or flat bread, meat, vegetables, beans, sweets and fruits. The flat bread, or pitta, is served at most meals and is used for dipping into pastes and salads. Steamed bulgur wheat is added to meat in many Syrian dishes, most notably kibbeh, which is a minced lamb main course and is considered to be one of Syria's national dishes. Garlic is used frequently and olive oil and purified butter are the main fats used. Also popular are houmous (chickpea and tahini dip) and falafel (fried ground chickpeas), as well as makkadem, which is a dish made from sheep's feet. In the Mediterranean Sea region of Syria, spiced yogurt is a speciality.

Meze, or small sampler-type dishes, such as alangi (stuffed vine leaves) and shanklish, a tangy sheep's cheese, are eaten regularly, as is a dish called muhammara, a spicy dip of chopped walnuts and red pepper, which is frequently served with chicken kebabs. Syrians also have a reputation for cheese making, particularly a stringy cheese called jibbneh mashallale, and for enjoying particularly sweet or particularly sour foods; they have the highest sugar consumption rate in the world.

Lebanon

The Western Asian Lebanese Republic, which is the smallest country in the Middle East, lies on the eastern shore of the Mediterranean Sea. Home to various cultures through the centuries, particularly the Persians, Greeks, Romans, Arabs and Ottoman Turks, as well as the French in more recent times, Lebanon's cuisine has taken elements from each of these civilizations. Lebanon experiences mild, wet winters and hot, dry summers and the locals rear goats in the inland rugged mountainous regions of the country.

The country's diverse culture is epitomized in its menus, from Greek and Turkish-type lamb dishes to the French influence on desserts, custards and croissants. Croissants stuffed with lamb, fish or chicken have evolved as a result of this French influence. Lebanese cuisine is also a mixture of the different specialities of each region and is considered to be a well-balanced, healthy diet, rich in fruit, vegetables, olive oil, herbs and spices. Muslims are forbidden to eat pork and it is not a popular meat with Lebanese Christians. Along the Mediterranean coast the country's capital and main seaport, Beirut, is renowned for its spicy fish (samkeh harra) and octopus (akhtabout). Lebanon also has a long history of olive oil production, with the different regions producing different types of olive and therefore slightly different versions of oil.

Throughout Lebanon the main ingredient of any recipe is freshness. They use seasonal fruit and vegetables rather than those grown in a greenhouse and the subtle use of herbs and spices, all of which are readily available in the souks (markets). One recipe that is well known in all regions of Lebanon is tabbouleh, made from parsley, mint, spring onions, tomatoes, bulgur wheat, lemon juice, olive oil and seasoning and served on a bed of lettuce.

Israel

Situated at the eastern edge of the Mediterranean Sea, Israel has deserts, mountain ranges and coastal plains, meaning temperatures vary enormously throughout the country. Along the temperate Mediterranean coastline, citrus fruit trees are grown, as are figs, pomegranates and olives. With a diverse culture and religious traditions, Jewish Israel has an equally diverse cuisine. Many Israeli recipes were brought by Jews originating in Asia and North Africa (Mizrahi Jews), whilst others were brought to the country by those emigrating from Eastern Europe and the western cultures and are more typical of traditional Jewish food from Hungary and Poland, as well as Russia.

Typical Israeli foods include flat bread, lentils, fresh fruits and nuts, stuffed vegetables, grilled lamb and beef, dairy products – including goat's cheese and many types of yogurt – and traditional spicy Mediterranean salads and spreads, such as fava bean spread. Some of the most typical dishes are stews, schnitzel (veal, chicken or turkey cutlets), cheese-filled crepes (blintzes), matzo balls (dumplings eaten with chicken soup) and latkes (potato pancakes). Sweets, made from honey and sesame seeds, are also popular.

A small percentage of Israel's recipes are kosher, meaning meat and milk products cannot be served during the same meal and the consumption of certain types of animals is banned. Basically, kosher meat must come from animals that have cleft hooves and chew their cud (so pork and other products that come from pigs are not to be eaten) and an animal must have been slaughtered quickly and under supervision of religious authorities for the meat to be considered kosher.

Main meals in Israel often start with a meze appetizer, which could include dips and stuffed vegetables. The soup and main course usually contains chicken or lamb, and fresh fruit or Middle Eastern pastries, such as baklava, are served as dessert.

Egypt

ट

The Arab Republic of Egypt is probably most famous for its ancient civilizations and the architectural treasures they left behind, such as the well-known pyramids at Giza, outside Cairo, and the tombs in the Valley of the Kings. The history of Egypt's food also stems from ancient times. Because of an incredibly dry climate the Ancient Eyptians relied on the flooding of the River Nile to irrigate their crops, which included wheat to make bread and barley to make beer. The Nile also produced fish, which provided the bulk of the protein for these ancient people, as the terrain was too dry and hot to rear livestock. The Ancient Egyptians were also fond of onion and garlic, a trend that has continued to the present day.

In addition to ancient traditions, foreign influence is evident in modern-day Egyptian dishes, particularly that of Turkey, making many recipes a mix of Mediterranean and Middle Eastern trends, such as the dessert baklava, which is drenched in honey, and Turkish coffee, which is drunk regularly. Influence also came from the Romans, the Arabs, the Ottoman Turks, the Syrians, the Lebanese and the Palestinians.

Egyptians enjoy houmous (chickpea and tahini dip) and aubergine dip, both eaten with pitta bread strips. Many of their dishes are simple, with naturally ripened fruits and vegetables mixed with fresh local spices, although not made too spicy or hot. Meat is eaten in moderation; it is cooked with vegetables and served with rice, salad or pasta. Weddings, festivals and ceremonies are a time for feasting on traditional Egyptian dishes, when popular meats like pigeon, chicken, mutton, camel and buffalo are eaten. As with most Mediterranean countries, food is about company and the Egyptians make meal times a definite family time. They eat fava beans regularly, honey is their traditional source of adding sweetness to dishes and most households make their own bread either from white flour or from wholemeal flour.

Libya

ℰ

Next along the coast from Egypt lies Libya. It seems that the Berbers, during the Neolithic period, were the first civilization to introduce farming and cattle rearing to ancient Libya. Subsequent occupations, particularly by the Phoenicians, the Greeks, the Persians, the Romans, the Vandals and the Byzantines have all left their mark on modern-day Libyan cuisine to a greater or lesser extent. Occupied by the Italians at the outbreak of the Second World War, much of Libya is desert, which means it has very high temperatures and very low rainfall.

Unsurprisingly, Libyan cuisine is a mix of Italian, Arabic and Mediterranean influences, with pasta dishes being popular, as well as the North African favourite of couscous, which in Libya is served with braised lamb, vegetables and dried fruit. Fruit is grown throughout Libya and in particular the country produces apricots, nectarines, grapes, peaches, melons and all types of citrus fruit. Libya tends to have national dishes, as opposed to regional ones, and, although they may be prepared in slightly different ways, the basic concept is the same across the country.

For religious reasons pork is not commonly served in Libya, and as a Muslim country there are many religious and national traditions about the way in which food is served and eaten. Food is served on a large platter and placed in the centre of the table so that all those eating can help themselves from the edge of the plate. The food in the centre of the plate is not eaten, but is offered to Heaven. Drinks are not served with meals, but a communal glass is handed around the table after the meal. Drinkers are not allowed to breathe until the glass has been removed from their lips.

Tunisia

The Republic of Tunisia has a diverse climate, with much of its southern region made up of the Sahara Desert. The Phoenicians, Romans, Vandals, Byzantines, Arabs, Spanish and French have all occupied Tunisia over the centuries. Though predominantly inherited from the nomadic tribes that originated in Tunisia, this series of conquests has affected the country's culture and the way its food is prepared and eaten.

Harissa, a hot, red pepper sauce, together with chilli peppers, garlic, olive oil, tomatoes and spices such as coriander and cumin play an important role in Tunisian cuisine. Compared to countries like Egypt and Libya, the Tunisians prefer their food spicy and hot. They eat a wide range of seafood and have many traditional lamb recipes.

The country has a long Mediterranean Sea coastline and many busy fishing ports, so the preparation of fish dishes varies enormously; grilled, baked, fried and coated in batter are all popular dishes. Most fish dishes are served with sliced lemon and a drizzle of olive oil, although squid, cuttlefish and octopus are often stuffed and served with Tunisia's national dish of couscous.

Tunisians cook their couscous in a type of steamer or double boiler, with the vegetables placed in the lower section and the grain in the top half. As the steam from the vegetables rises, so the couscous, made from the grain of semolina rice and ground wheat flour, is cooked. Couscous can be served with a variety of vegetables or with meats. In Tunisia it is usually served with lamb stew or broth. One traditional way in which Tunisians prepare young lamb is called 'coucha'. Shoulder of lamb is rubbed with olive oil, salt, mint, cayenne pepper and turmeric. The dish is oven-baked slowly in a tightly covered earthenware pot.

Algeria

The largest country on the Mediterranean Sea, the People's Republic of Algeria was formerly under Ottoman Turk rule but was invaded by the French in 1830 before it became independent in 1962. Most of Algeria's Mediterranean coastline is mountainous and the country's climate can range from extremely hot during the day to cool or chilly at night, with a high level of rainfall. Algeria's soil is very fertile and many locals are employed in the agriculture industry.

Algerian cuisine can trace its roots to a number of ancient cultures that once ruled, visited or traded with the country. Berber tribesmen marked the beginning of wheat cultivation, smen (cooked butter) and consumption of fruit such as dates; the Carthaginians created couscous; the Romans grew grain; Muslim Arabs introduced saffron, nutmeg, ginger, cloves and cinnamon from the 'Spice Islands' of Eastern Indonesia; and the French brought their breads.

Algerians prefer lamb, chicken or fish to be placed on a bed of warm couscous, accompanied by cooked vegetables such as carrots, chickpeas or tomatoes and they also enjoy spicy stews. They use couscous in desserts by adding a variety of ingredients, such as cinnamon, nutmeg, dates and figs (fig trees grow in abundance in the Algeria's desert regions). Bread is eaten with most meals and is usually French bread or flat bread like pitta.

As an Islamic nation, Algeria celebrates Ramadan each year. During this time they are not allowed to eat or drink between the hours of sunrise and sunset. At the end of Ramadan there is a feast comprising soup as a starter and lamb or beef as the main dish, although families living close to the Mediterranean Sea often substitute the meat with a fresh fish dish. Fresh fruit is usually served as the dessert at these celebrations.

Morocco

ℰ

T he Kingdom of Morocco gained its political independence from France in 1956. Bordered by the Strait of Gibraltar to the north and the Sahara Desert to the south, Morocco's coastal plains are rich and fertile and the climate is ideal for the agricultural industry.

With a very diverse cuisine, the country's choice of dishes has been heavily influenced over the centuries by the many different civilizations that have occupied it, namely the Berbers, the Spanish, the Corsicans, the Portuguese, the Moors, the Turks, the Arabs and the Jews. Home-grown citrus fruits, spices such as saffron, herbs such as mint and coriander and a plentiful supply of home-grown olives are all put to good use in Moroccan dishes. The country breeds sheep, cattle and poultry and uses the Mediterranean Sea as its plentiful source of fish. They use a number of spices to enhance the flavour of meat and fish dishes, including cinnamon, cumin, ginger, turmeric, paprika and sesame and anise seeds. Couscous is eaten regularly with vegetables, meat and fish and as a dessert.

Many Moroccan housewives make their own bread daily from semolina flour. It is prepared in the family's kitchen and marked before being sent to the bakery for cooking. Sweet Moroccan mint tea is usually taken with meals, although absinthe and pine nuts are added when mint is not plentiful. This is a green tea prepared for guests by the head of the family, although the way in which this ceremonial tea is prepared varies from one region to another. It is served in small glasses and skilfully poured from a height to give it a frothy head, returning the tea to the pot several times before serving it to the guest; this gives it a stronger flavour.

Starters *and*

Salads

With such a wonderful climate, it is little wonder that most of the Mediterranean countries can enjoy fresh produce throughout the year. Their salads, fruit and vegetables are virtually grown on their doorsteps, picked on the day of use and the flavours are out of this world. Mediterranean appetizers are not always used at the beginning of a meal, but often as a snack or to accompany drinks – think 'tapas' and 'antipasti'. The salads and starters covered here are irresistible.

Roasted Aubergine Dip
with Pitta Strips

Serves 6

4 pitta breads
2 large aubergines
1 garlic clove, peeled
$1/4$ tsp sesame oil
1 tbsp lemon juice
$1/2$ tsp ground cumin
salt and freshly ground
black pepper
2 tbsp freshly chopped parsley
fresh salad leaves, to serve

Preheat the oven to 180C˚/350˚F/Gas Mark 4. On a chopping board, cut the pitta breads into strips. Spread the bread in a single layer on a large baking sheet. Cook in the preheated oven for 15 minutes until golden and crisp. Leave to cool on a wire cooling rack.

Trim the aubergines, rinse lightly and reserve. Heat a griddle pan until almost smoking. Cook the aubergines and garlic for about 15 minutes. Turn the aubergines frequently, until very tender with wrinkled and charred skins. Remove from heat and leave to cool.

When the aubergines are cool enough to handle, cut in half and scoop out the cooked flesh and place in a food processor. Squeeze the softened garlic flesh from the papery skin and add to the aubergine. Blend the aubergine and garlic until smooth. Add the sesame oil, lemon juice and cumin and blend again to mix. Season to taste with salt and pepper, stir in the parsley.

Serve with the pitta strips and mixed salad leaves.

Italian Bean Soup

Serves 4

2 tsp olive oil
1 leek, washed and chopped
1 garlic clove, peeled and crushed
2 tsp dried oregano
75 g/3 oz green beans,
trimmed and cut into
bite-sized pieces
410 g/14 oz can cannellini beans,
drained and rinsed
75 g/3 oz small pasta shapes
1 litre/1³/₄ pint vegetable stock
8 cherry tomatoes
salt and freshly ground
black pepper
3 tbsp freshly shredded basil

Heat the oil in a large saucepan. Add the leek, garlic and oregano and cook gently for 5 minutes, stirring occasionally.

Stir in the green beans and the cannellini beans. Sprinkle in the pasta and pour in the stock.

Bring the stock mixture to the boil, then reduce the heat to a simmer.

Cook for 12–15 minutes, or until the vegetables are tender and the pasta is cooked to *al dente*. Stir occasionally.

In a heavy-based frying pan, dry-fry the tomatoes over a high heat until they soften and the skins begin to blacken. Gently crush the tomatoes in the pan with the back of a spoon and add to the soup.

Season to taste with salt and pepper. Stir in the shredded basil and serve immediately.

Mushroom Red Wine Pâté

Serves 4

3 large slices white bread,
crusts removed
2 tsp olive oil
1 small onion, peeled and
finely chopped
1 garlic clove, peeled and crushed
350 g/12 oz button mushrooms,
wiped and finely chopped
150 ml/¼ pint red wine
½ tsp dried mixed herbs
1 tbsp freshly chopped parsley
salt and freshly ground
black pepper
2 tbsp cream cheese

To serve:

finely chopped cucumber
finely chopped tomato

Preheat the oven to 180°C/350°F/Gas Mark 4. Cut the bread in half diagonally. Place the bread triangles on a baking tray and cook for 10 minutes.

Remove from the oven and split each bread triangle in half to make 12 triangles, then return to the oven until golden and crisp. Leave to cool on a wire rack.

Heat the oil in a saucepan and gently cook the onion and garlic until transparent.

Add the mushrooms and cook, stirring, for 3–4 minutes, or until the mushroom juices start to run.

Stir the wine and herbs into the mushroom mixture and bring to the boil. Reduce the heat and simmer uncovered until all the liquid is absorbed. Remove from the heat and season to taste with salt and pepper. Leave to cool.

When cold, beat in the soft cream cheese and adjust the seasoning. Place in a small clean bowl and chill until required. Serve the toast triangles with the cucumber and tomato.

Spanakopita (Greece)

Serves 4

50 g/2 oz melted butter, plus extra for greasing
275 g/10 oz filo pastry
salad, to serve

For the filling:

500 g/1 lb 1 oz fresh young leaf spinach, ready washed
2 tbsp olive oil
4 spring onions, trimmed and thinly sliced
3 tbsp chopped flat-leaf parsley
175 g/6 oz feta cheese, crumbled
3 eggs, beaten
2 tbsp double cream
salt and freshly ground black pepper
1 tbsp cumin seeds

Preheat the oven to 180°C/350°F/Gas Mark 4, 15 minutes before using. Grease a 25 x 18 x 7.5 cm/10 x 7 x 3 inch baking tin with melted butter.

Make the filling. Trim away any thick stalks from the spinach and chop the leaves into shreds. Heat the oil in a large, deep pan and fry the spring onions for 4 minutes to soften, then add the shredded spinach and stir to coat in the oil. Cook over a low heat for 5 minutes until the leaves collapse.

Lift the vegetables out of the pan with a slotted spoon, press out any excess liquid in a fine sieve, then place the drained leaves in a large mixing bowl to cool. When cold, add the chopped parsley, feta cheese, eggs and cream, then season with salt and pepper and stir together.

Line the prepared tin with a sheet of filo pastry, pressing well into the corners, then brush with melted butter. Cover with another sheet and continue to layer and butter the sheets until you have used half the pastry.

Spoon in the cooled filling and spread level, then place a filo sheet over the filling and brush with more melted butter. Continue layering and buttering until you have used up all the pastry. Mark into 12 slices with a sharp knife, sprinkle the top with a little water, then scatter over the cumin seeds. Bake for about 45 minutes until crisp and golden. Season with salt and pepper and serve the squares hot or cold with a fresh salad.

Spiced Couscous Vegetables

Serves 4

1 tbsp olive oil
1 large shallot, peeled and
finely chopped
1 garlic clove, peeled and
finely chopped
1 small red pepper, deseeded and
cut into strips
1 small yellow pepper, deseeded
and cut into strips
1 small aubergine, diced
1 tsp each turmeric, ground cumin,
ground cinnamon and paprika
2 tsp ground coriander
large pinch saffron strands
2 tomatoes, peeled, deseeded
and diced
2 tbsp lemon juice
225 g/8 oz couscous
225 ml/8 fl oz vegetable stock
2 tbsp raisins
2 tbsp whole almonds
2 tbsp freshly chopped parsley
2 tbsp freshly chopped coriander
salt and freshly ground black pepper

Heat the oil in a large frying pan and add the shallot and garlic and cook for 2–3 minutes until softened. Add the peppers and aubergine and reduce the heat.

Cook for 8–10 minutes until the vegetables are tender, adding a little water if necessary.

Test a piece of aubergine to ensure it is cooked through. Add all the spices and cook for a further minute, stirring.

Increase the heat and add the tomatoes and lemon juice. Cook for 2–3 minutes until the tomatoes have started to break down. Remove from the heat and leave to cool slightly.

Meanwhile, put the couscous into a large bowl. Bring the stock to the boil in a saucepan, then pour over the couscous. Stir well and cover with a clean tea towel.

Leave to stand for 7–8 minutes until all the stock is absorbed and the couscous is tender.

Uncover the couscous and fluff with a fork. Stir in the vegetable and spice mixture along with the raisins, almonds, parsley and coriander. Season to taste with salt and pepper and serve.

Bruschetta with Pecorino, Garlic Tomatoes

Serves 4

6 ripe but firm tomatoes
125 g/4 oz pecorino cheese, finely grated
1 tbsp oregano leaves
salt and freshly ground black pepper
3 tbsp olive oil
3 garlic cloves, peeled
8 slices of flat Italian bread, such as focaccia
50 g/2 oz mozzarella cheese
marinated black olives, to serve

Preheat grill and line the grill rack with tinfoil just before cooking. Make a small cross in the top of the tomatoes, then place in a small bowl and cover with boiling water. Leave to stand for 2 minutes, then drain and remove the skins.

Cut into quarters, remove the seeds, and chop the flesh into small dice. Mix the tomato flesh with the pecorino cheese and 2 teaspoons of the fresh oregano and season to taste with salt and pepper. Add 1 tablespoon of the olive oil and mix thoroughly.

Crush the garlic and spread evenly over the slices of bread. Heat 2 tablespoons of the olive oil in a large frying pan and sauté the bread slices until they are crisp and golden.

Place the fried bread on a lightly oiled baking tray and spoon on the tomato and cheese topping. Place a little mozzarella on top and place under the preheated grill for 3–4 minutes, until golden and bubbling. Garnish with the remaining oregano, then arrange the bruschettas on a serving plate and serve immediately with the olives.

Garlic Mushrooms

Serves 6

450 g/1 lb closed cup mushrooms
1 medium onion
4 garlic cloves
1 hot green chilli pepper (optional)
2 tbsp Spanish olive oil
150 ml/¹/₄ pint Spanish white wine
sea salt and freshly ground
black pepper
1 tbsp freshly chopped
flat-leaf parsley
warm chunky country bread,
to serve

Wipe the mushrooms with kitchen paper and trim the stalks. Reserve. Peel and chop the onion and garlic and slice the chilli, if using.

Heat the oil in a heavy-based frying pan and add the onion, garlic and chilli, if using, and gently fry for 5–6 minutes until beginning to soften, stirring occasionally. Add the mushrooms and cook, stirring frequently, until coated in the oil.

Pour in the white wine and bring to the boil. When the wine is bubbling, reduce the heat to a gentle simmer and cover with the lid. Cook for 10 minutes, or until the mushrooms are tender.

Add seasoning to taste, stir well, then spoon into a warm serving dish or casserole dish. Sprinkle with the chopped parsley and serve with chunks of warm country bread.

Aubergine Yogurt Dip

Makes 600 ml/1 pint

2 x 225 g/^{1}/$_2$ lb aubergines
1 tbsp light olive oil
1 tbsp lemon juice
2 garlic cloves, peeled and crushed
190 g/6.5 oz jar pimientos, drained
150 ml/^{1}/$_4$ pint natural yogurt
salt and freshly ground black pepper
25 g/1 oz black olives, pitted
and chopped
225 g/8 oz cauliflower florets
225 g/8 oz broccoli florets
125 g/4 oz carrots, peeled and
cut into 5 cm/2 inch strips

Preheat the oven to 200˚C/400˚F/Gas Mark 6. Pierce the skin of the aubergines with a fork and place on a baking tray. Cook for 40 minutes or until very soft. Cool the aubergines, then cut in half, scoop out the flesh and tip into a bowl.

Mash the aubergine with the olive oil, lemon juice and garlic until smooth or blend for a few seconds in a food processor. Chop the pimientos into small dice and add to the aubergine mixture.

When blended, add the yogurt. Stir well and season to taste with salt and pepper.

Add the chopped olives and leave in the refrigerator to chill for at least 30 minutes.

Place the cauliflower and broccoli florets and carrot strips into a frying pan and cover with boiling water. Simmer for 2 minutes, then rinse in cold water. Drain and serve as crudités to accompany the dip.

Wild Rice Dolmades (Greece)

Serves 4–6

6 tbsp olive oil
25g/1 oz pine nuts
175 g/6 oz mushrooms, wiped and finely chopped
4 spring onions, trimmed and finely chopped
1 garlic clove, peeled and crushed
50 g/2 oz cooked wild rice
2 tsp freshly chopped dill
2 tsp freshly chopped mint
salt and freshly ground black pepper
16–24 prepared medium vine leaves
about 300 ml/½ pint vegetable stock

To garnish:

lemon wedges
fresh dill sprigs

Heat 1 tbsp of the oil in a frying pan and gently cook the pine nuts for 2–3 minutes, stirring frequently, until golden. Remove from the pan and reserve.

Add 1½ tablespoons oil to the pan and gently cook the mushrooms, spring onions and garlic for 7–8 minutes until very soft. Stir in the rice, herbs, salt and pepper.

Put a heaped teaspoon of stuffing in the centre of each leaf (if the leaves are small, put two together, overlapping slightly). Fold over the stalk end, then the sides, and roll up to make a neat parcel. Continue until all the stuffing is used.

Arrange the stuffed leaves close together, seam-side down, in a large saucepan, drizzling each with a little of the remaining oil. There will be several layers. Pour over enough stock to cover. Put an inverted plate over the dolmades to stop them unrolling during cooking. Bring to the boil, then simmer very gently for 3 minutes. Cool in the saucepan.

Transfer the dolmades to a serving dish. Cover and chill in the refrigerator before serving. Sprinkle with the pine nuts and garnish with lemon and dill. Serve.

French Onion Tart

Serves 4

For the quick flaky pastry:

125 g/4¹/2 oz butter
175 g/6 oz plain flour
a pinch salt

For the filling:

2 tbsp olive oil
4 large onions, peeled and
thinly sliced
3 tbsp white wine vinegar
2 tbsp muscovado sugar
175 g/6 oz Cheddar cheese, grated
some beaten egg or milk
salt and freshly ground black pepper

Preheat the oven to 200°C/400°F/Gas Mark 6. Place the butter in the freezer for 30 minutes. Sift the flour and salt into a large bowl. Grate the butter on the coarse side of a grater, dipping it in the flour to make it easier to grate. Mix the butter into the flour, using a palette knife, making sure all the butter is coated with flour. Add 2 tablespoons cold water and continue to mix, bringing the mixture together. Use your hands to complete the mixing. Add a little more water if needed to leave a clean bowl. Place the dough in a polythene bag and chill in the refrigerator for 30 minutes.

Heat the oil in a large frying pan, then fry the onions for 10 minutes, stirring occasionally, until softened. Stir in the white wine vinegar and muscovado sugar. Increase the heat and stir frequently for another 4–5 minutes until the onions turn a deep caramel colour. Cook for another 5 minutes, then reserve to cool.

On a lightly floured surface, roll out the pastry dough to a 35 cm/14 inch round. Wrap over a rolling pin and lift the round onto a baking sheet. Sprinkle half the cheese over the dough, leaving a 5 cm/2 inch border around the edge, then spoon the caramelized onions over the cheese. Fold the uncovered dough edges over the edge of the filling to form a rim. Brush the rim with beaten egg or milk. Season to taste with salt and pepper. Sprinkle over the remaining cheese and bake for 20–25 minutes. Transfer to a large plate and serve immediately.

Olive Feta Parcels

Makes 30

1 small red and 1 small
yellow pepper
125 g/4^1/$_2$ oz assorted marinated
green and black olives
125 g/4^1/$_2$ oz feta cheese
2 tbsp pine nuts, lightly toasted
6 sheets filo pastry
3 tbsp olive oil
sour cream and chive dip,
to serve

Preheat the oven to 180°C/350°F/Gas Mark 4. Preheat the grill, then line the rack with kitchen foil.

Cut the peppers into quarters and remove the seeds. Place skin-side up on the foil-lined rack and cook under the preheated grill for 10 minutes, turning occasionally until the skins begin to blacken. Place the peppers in a polythene bag and leave until cool enough to handle, then skin and thinly slice. Chop the olives and cut the feta cheese into small cubes. Mix together the olives, feta, sliced peppers and pine nuts.

Cut a sheet of pastry in half, then brush with a little of the oil. Place a spoonful of the olive and feta mix about one-third of the way up the pastry sheet. Fold over the pastry and wrap to form a square package encasing the filling completely. Place this package in the centre of the second half of the pastry sheet.

Brush the edges lightly with a little oil, bring up the corners to meet in the centre and twist them loosely to form a pocket. Brush with a little more oil and repeat with the remaining pastry sheets and filling.

Place the pockets on a lightly oiled baking sheet and bake in the preheated oven for 10–15 minutes, or until crisp and golden brown. Serve with the dip.

Greek Salad

Serves 4

1 medium red onion
$^1/_2$ cucumber
4 ripe medium tomatoes
175 g/6 oz feta cheese
50 g/2 oz Kalamata olives or large
black olives, preferably pitted
2–3 lemon thyme sprigs
2 tbsp Greek extra virgin olive oil

Health Tip:

Using olive oil, especially extra virgin
olive oil, is extremely good for you, as
it helps to boost the immune system
and to protect the body against
viruses. It is also reputed to help in
the fight against various diseases, such
as cancer and heart disease.

Peel the onion and cut in half, then cut in half again and slice thinly to form half moons. Reserve.

Peel the cucumber and cut into small pieces. Rinse the tomatoes and cut into wedges and reserve both.

Drain the cheese and cut into small cubes.

Mix all the prepared ingredients together in a large bowl, then divide between four individual bowls or plates. Arrange the olives on top. Shred a little of the lemon thyme over and drizzle with the olive oil. Garnish with the remaining thyme and serve.

Bulghur Wheat Salad with Minty Lemon Dressing

Serves 4

125 g/4 oz bulghur wheat
10 cm /4 inch piece cucumber
2 shallots, peeled
125 g/4 oz baby sweetcorn
3 ripe but firm tomatoes

Dressing:

grated rind of 1 lemon
3 tbsp lemon juice
3 tbsp freshly chopped mint
2 tbsp freshly chopped parsley
1–2 tsp clear honey
2 tbsp sunflower oil
salt and freshly ground
black pepper

Place the bulghur wheat in a saucepan and cover with boiling water.

Simmer for about 10 minutes, then drain thoroughly and turn into a serving bowl.

Cut the cucumber into small dice, chop the shallots finely and reserve. Steam the sweetcorn over a pan of boiling water for 10 minutes or until tender. Drain and slice into thick chunks.

Cut a cross on the top of each tomato and place in boiling water until their skins start to peel away.

Remove the skins and the seeds and cut the tomatoes into small dice.

Make the dressing by briskly whisking all the ingredients in a small bowl until mixed well.

When the bulghur wheat has cooled a little, add all the prepared vegetables and stir in the dressing. Season to taste with salt and pepper and serve.

Garlic Wild Mushroom Galettes

Serves 6

1 quantity quick flaky pastry
(*see* French Onion Tart,
page 90), chilled
1 onion, peeled and thinly sliced
275 g/10 oz mixed mushrooms, e.g.
oyster, chestnut,
morels, chanterelles
25 g/1 oz butter
1 red chilli, deseeded and
thinly sliced
2 garlic cloves, peeled and very
thinly sliced
2 tbsp freshly chopped parsley
125 g/4¹/₂ oz mozzarella
cheese, sliced

To serve:

cherry tomatoes
mixed green salad leaves

Preheat the oven to 220°C/425°F/Gas Mark 7. On a lightly floured surface, roll out the chilled flaky pastry very thinly. Cut out 6 x 15 cm/6 inch circles and place on a lightly oiled baking sheet.

Divide the onion into rings and reserve. Wipe or lightly rinse the mushrooms. Half or quarter any large mushrooms and keep the small ones whole. Heat the butter in a frying pan and fry the onion, chilli and garlic gently for about 3 minutes. Add the mushrooms and cook for about 5 minutes, or until beginning to soften.

Stir the parsley into the mushroom mixture and drain off any excess liquid. Pile the mushroom mixture onto the pastry circles within 5 mm/¹/₄ inch of the edges. Arrange the sliced mozzarella cheese on top. Bake in the preheated oven for 12–15 minutes, or until golden brown, and serve with the tomatoes and salad.

Panzanella (Italy)

Serves 4

250 g/9 oz day-old Italian-style bread
1 tbsp red wine vinegar
4 tbsp olive oil
1 tsp lemon juice
1 small garlic clove, peeled and
finely chopped
1 red onion, peeled and finely sliced
1 cucumber, peeled if preferred
225 g/8 oz ripe tomatoes, deseeded
150 g/5 oz pitted black olives
about 20 basil leaves, coarsely torn
or left whole if small
sea salt and freshly ground
black pepper

Cut the bread into thick slices, leaving the crusts on. Add 1 teaspoon of red wine vinegar to a jug of iced water, put the slices of bread in a bowl and pour over the water. Make sure the bread is covered completely. Leave to soak for 3–4 minutes until just soft.

Remove the soaked bread from the water and squeeze it gently, first with your hands and then in a clean tea towel to remove any excess water. Put the bread on a plate, cover with clingfilm and chill in the refrigerator for about 1 hour.

Meanwhile, whisk together the olive oil, the remaining red wine vinegar and lemon juice in a large serving bowl. Add the garlic and onion and stir to coat well.

Halve the cucumber and remove the seeds. Chop both the cucumber and tomatoes into 1 cm/^{1}/$_2$ inch dice. Add to the garlic and onions with the olives. Tear the bread into bite-sized chunks and add to the bowl with the fresh basil leaves. Toss together to mix and serve immediately, with a grinding of sea salt and black pepper.

Falafel Salad with Houmous Olives

Serves 4

For the falafels:
225 g/8 oz dried chickpeas, soaked
overnight in cold water, or use canned
11 tbsp tahini paste
1 garlic clove, peeled and crushed
salt and freshly ground black pepper
1 tsp ground turmeric
$^1/_2$–1 tsp ground cumin
1 tsp ground coriander
$^1/_4$ tsp cayenne pepper, or to taste
2 tbsp freshly chopped mint
2 tbsp freshly chopped coriander
1 tbsp plain white flour
2 tbsp vegetable oil
125 g/4 oz assorted salad leaves
50 g/2 oz green olives

For the houmous:
400 g/14 oz can chickpeas
2–3 tbsp lemon juice
1 garlic clove, peeled
4 tbsp tahini paste
salt and freshly ground black pepper

Drain the chickpeas and, if using dried chickpeas, place in a saucepan and completely cover with water. Bring to the boil and remove any scum that rises to the surface. Reduce the heat and simmer for 40 minutes, or until tender, then drain.

Place the chickpeas in a food processor, add the tahini paste and garlic and whizz until the chickpeas are roughly chopped. Add the seasoning, herbs and spices and whiz until the mixture comes together. Scrape into a bowl, cover lightly and leave for 30 minutes before shaping into small patties.

Meanwhile, make the houmous by placing all the ingredients, except the lemon juice, in a food processor and whizzing until smooth. Add enough lemon juice to make a dipping consistency.

When ready to serve, dust the falafel patties in the flour. Heat a little oil in a frying pan and fry over a medium heat for 4–6 minutes until they are heated through and crisp. Drain on absorbent kitchen paper.

Lightly rinse the salad leaves and arrange in a serving dish. Place the falafels on top together with the olives and serve with the houmous.

Mediterranean Potato Salad

Serves 4

700 g/1¹/₂ lb small waxy potatoes
2 red onions, peeled and
roughly chopped
1 yellow pepper, deseeded and
roughly chopped
1 green pepper, deseeded and
roughly chopped
6 tbsp extra virgin olive oil
125 g/4¹/₂ oz ripe tomatoes, chopped
50 g/2 oz pitted black olives, sliced
125 g/4¹/₂ oz feta cheese
3 tbsp freshly chopped parsley
2 tbsp white wine vinegar
1 tsp Dijon mustard
1 tsp clear honey
salt and freshly ground black pepper
sprigs fresh parsley, to garnish

Preheat the oven to 200°C/400°F/Gas Mark 6. Place the potatoes in a large saucepan of salted water, bring to the boil and simmer until just tender. Do not overcook. Drain and plunge into cold water, to stop them from cooking further.

Place the onions in a bowl with the peppers. Pour over 2 tablespoons of the olive oil. Stir and spoon onto a large baking tray. Cook in the preheated oven for 25–30 minutes, or until the vegetables are tender and lightly charred in places, stirring occasionally. Remove from the oven and transfer to a large bowl.

Cut the potatoes into bite-sized pieces and mix with the roasted onions and peppers. Add the tomatoes and olives to the potatoes. Crumble over the feta cheese and sprinkle with the chopped parsley.

Whisk together the remaining olive oil, vinegar, mustard and honey, then season to taste with salt and pepper. Pour the dressing over the potatoes and toss gently together. Garnish with parsley sprigs and serve immediately.

Roasted Red Pepper, Tomato Red Onion Soup

Serves 4

fine spray of olive oil
2 large red peppers, deseeded
and roughly chopped
1 red onion, peeled and
roughly chopped
3 tomatoes, halved
1 small crusty French loaf
1 garlic clove, peeled
600 ml/1 pint vegetable stock
salt and freshly ground
black pepper
1 tsp Worcestershire sauce
4 tbsp fromage frais/sour cream

Preheat the oven to 190°C/375°F/Gas Mark 5. Spray a large roasting tin with the oil and place the peppers and onion in the base. Cook in the oven for 10 minutes. Add the tomatoes and cook for a further 20 minutes, or until the peppers are soft.

Cut the bread into 1 cm/¹/₂ inch slices. Cut the garlic clove in half and rub the cut edge over the bread.

Place all the bread slices on a large baking sheet and bake in the preheated oven for 10 minutes, turning halfway through, until golden and crisp.

Remove the vegetables from the oven and allow to cool slightly, then blend in a food processor until smooth. Strain the vegetable mixture through a large nylon sieve into a saucepan, to remove the seeds and skin. Add the stock, season to taste with salt and pepper and stir to mix. Heat the soup gently until piping hot.

In a small bowl, beat together the Worcestershire sauce with the fromage frais/sour cream. Pour the soup into warmed bowls and swirl a spoonful of the fromage frais mixture into each bowl. Serve immediately with the garlic toast.

Chorizo & Padrón Pepper Pinchos (Spain)

Serves 4

175 g/6 oz Padrón peppers
2 tbsp Spanish olive oil
sea salt
1 baguette, cut into slices
225 g/8 oz chorizo sausages

Lightly rinse the peppers and dry on absorbent kitchen paper.

Heat the oil in a frying pan and, when hot, add the rinsed and dried peppers. Cook, stirring frequently, for 8–10 minutes until the skins on all the peppers have blistered. Remove the peppers from the frying pan and place on a plate lined with absorbent kitchen paper. Sprinkle with a little sea salt. Reserve. In the meantime, cook the chorizo sausages in the frying pan.

Sprinkle the bread with a little Spanish extra virgin olive oil and arrange the Padrón peppers on top with the chorizo. Pin together with a cocktail stick and serve.

Antipasti with Focaccia

Serves 4

3 fresh figs, quartered
125 g/4 oz green beans, cooked
and halved
1 small head of radicchio, rinsed
and shredded
125 g/4 oz large prawns, peeled
and cooked
125 can sardines, drained
25 g/1 oz pitted black olives
25 g/1 oz stuffed green olives
125 g/4 oz mozzarella cheese, sliced
50 g/2 oz Italian salami sausage,
thinly sliced
3 tbsp olive oil
275 g/10 oz strong white flour
pinch of sugar
3 tsp easy-blend quick-acting yeast
or 15 g/¹/₂ oz fresh yeast
175 g/6 oz fine semolina
1 tsp salt
300 ml/¹/₂ pint warm water
a little extra olive oil for brushing
1 tbsp coarse salt crystals

Preheat oven to 220˚C/ 425˚F/Gas Mark 7, 15 minutes before baking.
Arrange the fresh fruit, vegetables, prawns, sardines, olives, cheese and
meat on a large serving platter. Drizzle over 1 tablespoon of the olive oil,
then cover and chill in the refrigerator while making the bread.

Sift the flour, sugar, semolina and salt into a large mixing bowl then
sprinkle in the dried yeast. Make a well in the centre and add the
remaining 2 tablespoons of olive oil. Add the warm water, a little at a
time, and mix together until a smooth, pliable dough is formed. If using
fresh yeast, cream the yeast with the sugar, then gradually beat in half
the warm water. Leave in a warm place until frothy then proceed as for
dried yeast.

Place on to a lightly floured board and knead until smooth and elastic.
Place the dough in a lightly greased bowl, cover and leave in a warm
place for 45 minutes.

Knead again and flatten the dough into a large, flat oval shape about
1 cm/¹/₂ inch thick. Place on a lightly oiled baking tray. Prick the surface
with the end of a wooden spoon and brush with olive oil. Sprinkle on the
coarse salt and bake in the preheated oven for 25 minutes, or until
golden. Serve the bread with the prepared platter of food.

Kofte (Turkey)

Serves 4

500 g/1 lb 1 oz lean minced lamb
1 onion, peeled and finely chopped
1 small red chilli, deseeded and
finely chopped
1 medium egg, beaten
$1/4$ tsp ground cumin
$1/4$ tsp ground cinnamon
salt and freshly ground black pepper
1 tbsp olive oil

To serve:

2 large ripe tomatoes, sliced
1 ripe avocado, peeled, pitted
and cubed
rocket leaves
225 g/8 oz couscous, cooked
4 tbsp freshly chopped coriander
1 lemon, cut into wedges

Place the minced lamb, onion, chilli, beaten egg and spices in a bowl. Season with salt and pepper, then blend the mixture in a food processor or bring the mixture together with your hands until evenly combined.

Divide the mixture into 16 equal pieces and roll these into balls. Thread two balls onto each of the soaked skewers, moulding into oval shapes and leaving a space in between them.

Line a grill rack with kitchen foil and preheat the grill to medium. Brush the meatballs lightly with the olive oil, then place the skewers under the grill and cook for about 15 minutes, turning them regularly, until browned.

Arrange the tomatoes, avocado, rocket leaves and couscous between four plates. Top each with two skewers of meatballs, then serve sprinkled with chopped coriander and lemon wedges.

Mediterranean Chowder

Serves 6

1 tbsp olive oil
1 tbsp butter
1 large onion, peeled and
finely sliced
4 celery stalks, trimmed and
thinly sliced
2 garlic cloves, peeled and crushed
1 bird's-eye chilli, deseeded and
finely chopped
1 tbsp plain flour
225 g/8 oz potatoes, peeled
and diced
600 ml/1 pint fish or vegetable stock
700 g/1$\frac{1}{2}$ lb whiting or cod fillet
cut into 2.5 cm/1 inch cubes
2 tbsp freshly chopped parsley
125 g/4 oz large peeled prawns
198 g/7 oz can sweetcorn, drained
salt and freshly ground black pepper
150 ml/$\frac{1}{4}$ pint single cream
1 tbsp freshly snipped chives
warm, crusty bread, to serve

Heat the oil and butter together in a large saucepan, add the onion, celery and garlic and cook gently for 2–3 minutes until softened. Add the chilli and stir in the flour. Cook, stirring, for a further minute.

Add the potatoes to the saucepan with the stock. Bring to the boil, cover and simmer for 10 minutes. Add the fish cubes to the saucepan with the chopped parsley and cook for a further 5–10 minutes, or until the fish and potatoes are just tender.

Stir in the peeled prawns and sweetcorn and season to taste with salt and pepper. Pour in the cream and adjust the seasoning, if necessary.

Scatter the snipped chives over the top of the chowder. Ladle into 6 large bowls and serve immediately with plenty of warm crusty bread.

Niçoise Salad

Serves 4

1 small iceberg lettuce
225 g/8 oz French beans
225 g/8 oz baby new
potatoes, scrubbed
4 eggs
1 green pepper
1 onion, peeled
200 g/7 oz can tuna in water, drained
and flaked into small pieces
50 g/2 oz hard cheese, cut
into small cubes (optional)
8 ripe but firm cherry tomatoes, quartered
50 g/2 oz black pitted olives, halved
freshly chopped basil, to garnish

For the lime vinaigrette:

3 tbsp olive oil
2 tbsp white wine vinegar
4 tbsp lime juice and
grated rind of 1 lime
1 tsp Dijon mustard
1–2 tsp caster sugar
salt and freshly ground black pepper

Cut the lettuce into four and remove the hard core. Tear into bite-sized pieces and arrange on a large serving platter or four individual plates.

Cook the French beans in boiling salted water for 8 minutes and the potatoes for 10 minutes, or until tender. Drain and rinse in cold water until cool, then cut both the beans and potatoes in half with a sharp knife.

Boil the eggs for 10 minutes, then rinse thoroughly under a cold running tap until cool. Remove the shells under water and cut each egg into four. Remove the seeds from the pepper and cut into thin strips and finely chop the onion.

Arrange the beans, potatoes, eggs, peppers and onion on top of the lettuce. Add the tuna, cheese (if using) and tomatoes. Sprinkle the olives over and garnish with the basil.

To make the vinaigrette, place all the ingredients in a screw-topped jar and shake vigorously until everything is thoroughly mixed. Spoon 4 tablespoons over the top of the prepared salad and serve the remainder separately.

Salt Cod Fritters

Serves 4

350 g/12 oz salt cod
450 g/1 lb potatoes, preferably a
floury variety such as King Edward,
peeled and chopped
240 ml/8 fl oz milk
1 onion, peeled and chopped
5 tsp Spanish olive oil, plus
150 ml/1¼ pint for frying
1½ tbsp freshly chopped parsley
2 tbsp lemon juice
freshly ground black pepper
2 medium eggs
2 tbsp plain white flour
100 g/3½ oz dried
white breadcrumbs
allioli and lemon wedges, to serve

Place the cod in a bowl and cover with cold water. Leave for at least 24 hours, or until dehydrated, changing the water frequently. Drain and pat dry.

Cook the potatoes in boiling water for 15 minutes, or until tender. Drain and mash.

Pour the milk into a pan and add half the onion and the cod. Poach for 10 minutes, or until tender, then remove, cool and discard the skin and bones. Flake into pieces and place in a bowl. Beat in the oil, then stir in a little potato, the remaining onion and the parsley. Gradually beat in the remaining potato, lemon juice, pepper and 1 egg.

Chill in the refrigerator, then shape into about 16 cakes and chill for 1 hour.

Dip the fritters into the flour, then the other beaten egg and coat in the breadcrumbs. Fry in the oil for 4 minutes, or until crisp, turning halfway through cooking. Drain and serve with the allioli and lemon wedges.

Mediterranean Rice Salad

Serves 4

250 g/9 oz Camargue red rice
2 sun-dried tomatoes, finely chopped
2 garlic cloves, peeled and finely chopped
4 tbsp oil from a jar of sun-dried tomatoes
2 tsp balsamic vinegar
2 tsp red wine vinegar
salt and freshly ground black pepper
1 red onion, peeled and thinly sliced
1 yellow pepper, quartered and deseeded
1 red pepper, quartered and deseeded
1/2 cucumber, peeled and diced
6 ripe plum tomatoes, cut into wedges
1 fennel bulb, halved and thinly sliced
fresh basil leaves, to garnish

Cook the rice in a saucepan of lightly salted boiling water for 35–40 minutes, or until tender. Drain well and reserve.

Whisk the sun-dried tomatoes, garlic, oil and vinegars together in a small bowl or jug. Season to taste with salt and pepper. Put the sliced red onion in a large bowl, pour over the dressing and leave to allow the flavours to develop.

Put the peppers skin-side up on a grill rack and cook under a preheated hot grill for 5–6 minutes, or until blackened and charred. Remove and place in a polythene bag (the moisture will help loosen the skins). When cool enough to handle, peel off the skins and slice the flesh.

Add the peppers, cucumber, tomatoes, fennel and rice to the onions. Mix gently together to coat in the dressing. Cover and chill in the refrigerator for 30 minutes to allow the flavours to mingle.

Remove the salad from the refrigerator and leave to stand at room temperature for 20 minutes. Garnish with fresh basil leaves and serve.

Fried Whitebait with Rocket Salad

Serves 4

450 g/1 lb whitebait, fresh or frozen
oil, for frying
85 g/3 oz plain flour
$^1/_2$ tsp of cayenne pepper
salt and freshly ground black pepper

For the salad:

125 g/4 oz rocket leaves
125 g/4 oz cherry tomatoes, halved
75 g/3 oz cucumber, cut into dice
3 tbsp olive oil
1 tbsp fresh lemon juice
$^1/_2$ tsp Dijon mustard
$^1/_2$ tsp caster sugar

If the whitebait are frozen, thaw completely, then wipe dry with absorbent kitchen paper.

Start to heat the oil in a deep-fat fryer. Arrange the fish in a large, shallow dish and toss well in the flour, cayenne pepper and salt and pepper.

Deep fry the fish in batches for 2–3 minutes, or until crisp and golden. Keep the cooked fish warm while deep frying the remaining fish.

Meanwhile, to make the salad, arrange the rocket leaves, cherry tomatoes and cucumber on individual serving dishes. Whisk the olive oil and the remaining ingredients together and season lightly. Drizzle the dressing over the salad and serve with the whitebait.

Quick Mediterranean Prawns

Serves 4

20 raw Mediterranean prawns
3 tbsp olive oil
1 garlic clove, peeled and crushed
finely grated zest and juice
of 1/2 lemon
fresh rosemary sprigs

For the pesto and
sun-dried tomato dips:

150 ml/1/4 pint Greek style
1 tbsp prepared pesto
150 ml/1/4 pint crème fraîche
1 tbsp sun-dried tomato paste
1 tbsp wholegrain mustard
salt and freshly ground
black pepper
lemon wedges, to garnish

Remove the shells from the prawns, leaving the tail shells. Using a small sharp knife, remove the dark vein that runs along the back of the prawns. Rinse and drain on absorbent paper towels.

Whisk 2 tablespoons of the oil with the garlic, lemon zest and juice in a small bowl. Bruise 1 sprig rosemary with a rolling pin and add to the bowl. Add the prawns, toss to coat, then cover and leave to marinate in the refrigerator until needed.

For the simple dips, mix the yogurt and pesto in one bowl and the crème fraîche, tomato paste and mustard in another bowl. Season to taste with salt and pepper.

Heat a wok, add the remaining oil and swirl round to coat the sides. Remove the prawns from the marinade, leaving any juices and the rosemary behind. Add to the wok and stir-fry over a high heat for 3–4 minutes, or until the prawns are pink and just cooked through.

Remove the prawns from the wok and arrange on a platter. Garnish with lemon wedges and more fresh rosemary sprigs and serve hot or cold with the dips.

Calamares (Spain)

Serves 4

450 g/1 lb small squid
2–3 tbsp plain flour
sea salt and freshly ground
black pepper
4 medium egg whites
125 g/4 oz cornflour
about 600 ml/1 pint oil,
for deep frying
salad leaves and lemon wedges
(optional), to serve

Cook's tip:

If liked, after cleaning the squid,
rather than cutting into rings, cut
the squid into 5 cm/2 inch pieces
and score a diamond pattern
over the inside of each piece. Fry
these in the same manner.

Clean the squid if necessary and cut into rings. Rinse lightly and pat dry with absorbent kitchen paper. Place the flour in a polythene bag and add seasoning to taste. Add the squid rings to the bag and shake lightly until the squid is lightly coated in the flour. Reserve while making the batter.

Lightly whisk the egg whites until frothy, then gradually add 1–2 tablespoons of the cornflour, beating well after each addition. Continue adding the cornflour and beating well until a light coating batter is achieved.

Heat the oil for deep frying in a large saucepan or deep-fat fryer to 180°C/350°F. Place 2 or 3 squid rings in the batter and coat lightly. Remove with a slotted spoon, allowing any excess batter to drip back into the bowl.

Carefully lower the squid rings into the hot oil and cook for 30 seconds, or until golden brown and crisp. Remove and drain on absorbent kitchen paper. Repeat until all the batter has been used. Keep the cooked squid warm in a low oven until all the rings have been cooked. Serve on a bed of salad leaves with lemon to squeeze over, if liked.

Griddled Garlic Lemon Squid

Serves 4

125 g/4 oz long-grain rice
300 ml/$^1/_2$ pint fish stock
225 g/8 oz squid, cleaned
finely grated zest of 1 lemon
1 garlic clove, peeled and crushed
1 shallot, peeled and finely chopped
2 tbsp freshly chopped coriander
2 tbsp lemon juice
salt and freshly ground black pepper

Rinse the rice until the water runs clear, then place in a saucepan with the stock. Bring to the boil, then reduce the heat. Cover and simmer gently for 10 minutes.

Turn off the heat and leave the pan covered so the rice can steam while you cook the squid.

Remove the tentacles from the squid and reserve. Cut the body cavity in half. Using the tip of a small sharp knife, score the inside flesh of the body cavity in a diamond pattern. Do not cut all the way through.

Mix the lemon zest, crushed garlic and chopped shallot together. Place the squid in a shallow bowl and sprinkle over the lemon mixture and stir.

Heat a griddle pan until almost smoking. Cook the squid for 3–4 minutes until cooked through, then slice.

Sprinkle with the coriander and lemon juice. Season to taste with salt and pepper. Drain the rice and serve immediately with the squid.

Mussels with Creamy Garlic Saffron Sauce

Serves 4

700 g/1¹/₂ lb fresh live mussels
300 ml/¹/₂ pint good-quality
dry white wine
1 tbsp olive oil
1 shallot, peeled and finely chopped
2 garlic cloves, peeled and crushed
1 tbsp freshly chopped oregano
2 saffron strands
150 ml/¹/₄ pint single cream
salt and freshly ground black pepper
fresh crusty bread, to serve

Clean the mussels thoroughly in plenty of cold water and remove any beards and barnacles from the shells. Discard any mussels that are open or damaged. Place in a large bowl and cover with cold water and leave in the refrigerator until required, if prepared earlier.

Pour the wine into a large saucepan and bring to the boil. Tip the mussels into the pan, cover and cook, shaking the saucepan periodically for 6–8 minutes, or until the mussels have opened completely.

Discard any mussels with closed shells, then using a slotted spoon, carefully remove the remaining open mussels from the saucepan and keep them warm. Reserve the cooking liquor.

Heat the olive oil in a small frying pan and cook the shallot and garlic gently for 2–3 minutes, until softened. Add the reserved cooking liquid and chopped oregano and cook for a further 3–4 minutes. Stir in the saffron and the cream and heat through gently. Season to taste with salt and pepper. Place a few mussels in individual serving bowls and spoon over the saffron sauce. Serve immediately with plenty of fresh crusty bread.

Meat & Poultry

Though seafood might be what first comes to mind when considering the Mediterranean, the countries in this region like their meat as much as anybody. The terrain, the lushness of the vegetation and other factors will determine how adept a country's locals are at rearing livestock. Goat and lamb are equals flavour-wise when they are cooked well, and goat is often substituted for lamb – which would work well in Lamb and Potato Moussaka.

Lamb Potato Moussaka (Greece)

Serves 6

4–6 potatoes, peeled
125 g/4¹/₂ oz plus 1 tbsp butter
1 large onion, peeled and chopped
2–4 garlic cloves, peeled
and crushed
700 g/1¹/₂ lb cooked roast lamb,
trimmed and cubed
3 tbsp tomato puree
1 tbsp freshly chopped parsley
salt and freshly ground
black pepper
3–4 tbsp olive oil
2 aubergines, trimmed and sliced
4 tomatoes, sliced
2 eggs
300 ml/¹/₂ pint Greek yogurt
2–3 tbsp grated Parmesan cheese

Preheat the oven to 200°C/400°F/Gas Mark 6, about 15 minutes before required. Thinly slice the potatoes and rinse thoroughly in cold water, then pat dry with a clean dishtowel.

Melt 50 g/2 oz of the butter in a frying pan and fry the potatoes, in batches, until crisp and golden. Using a slotted spoon, remove from the pan and reserve. Use one third of the potatoes to line the base of an ovenproof dish.

Add the onion and garlic to the butter remaining in the pan and cook for 5 minutes. Add the lamb and fry for 1 minute. Blend the tomato puree with 3 tablespoons water and stir into the pan with the parsley and salt and pepper. Spoon over the layer of potatoes, then top with the remaining potato slices.

Heat the oil and the remaining butter in the pan and brown the aubergine slices for 5–6 minutes. Arrange the tomatoes on top of the potatoes, then the aubergines on top of the tomatoes. Beat the eggs with the yogurt and Parmesan cheese. Pour over the aubergine and tomatoes. Bake in the preheated oven for 25 minutes, or until golden and piping hot. Serve.

Moroccan Lamb with Apricots

Serves 6

5 cm/2 inch piece root ginger,
peeled and grated

3 garlic cloves, peeled and crushed

1 tsp ground cardamom

1 tsp ground cumin

2 tbsp olive oil

450 g/1 lb lamb neck
fillet, cubed

1 large red onion, peeled
and chopped

400 g/14 oz can chopped tomatoes

125 g/4 oz ready-to-eat
dried apricots

400 g/14 oz can chickpeas, drained

7 large sheets filo pastry

50 g/2 oz butter, melted

pinch nutmeg

dill sprigs, to garnish

Preheat the oven to 190°C/375°F/Gas Mark 5. Pound the ginger, garlic, cardamom and cumin to a paste with a pestle and mortar. Heat 1 tablespoon of the oil in a large frying pan and fry the spice paste for 3 minutes. Remove and reserve.

Add the remaining oil and fry the lamb in batches for about 5 minutes until golden brown. Return all the lamb to the pan and add the onions and spice paste. Fry for 10 minutes, stirring occasionally. Add the chopped tomatoes, cover and simmer for 15 minutes. Add the apricots and chickpeas and simmer for a further 15 minutes.

Lightly oil a round 18 cm/7 inch spring-form cake tin. Lay one sheet of pastry in the base of the tin, allowing the excess to fall over the sides. Brush with melted butter, then layer five more sheets in the tin and brush each one with butter. Spoon in the filling and level the surface. Layer half the remaining pastry sheets on top, again brushing each with butter. Fold the overhanging pastry over the top of the filling. Brush the remaining sheet with butter and scrunch up and place on top of the pie so that the whole pie is completely covered. Brush with melted butter once more. Bake in the preheated oven for 45 minutes, then reserve for 10 minutes. Unclip the tin and remove the pie. Sprinkle with the nutmeg, garnish with the dill sprigs and serve.

Lamb ❧ Date Tagine (Morocco)

Serves 4

few saffron strands
1 tbsp olive oil
1 onion, peeled and cut into wedges
2–3 garlic cloves, peeled and sliced
550 g/1¼ lb lean lamb such as
neck fillet, diced
1 cinnamon stick, bruised
1 tsp ground cumin
225 g/8 oz carrots, peeled
and sliced
350 g/12 oz sweet potato,
peeled and diced
900 ml/1½ pints lamb or
vegetable stock
salt and freshly ground
black pepper
100 g/4 oz dates (fresh or dried),
pitted and halved
freshly prepared couscous, to serve

Place the saffron in a small bowl, cover with warm water and leave to infuse for 10 minutes. Heat the oil in a large, heavy-based pan, add the onion, garlic and lamb and sauté for 8–10 minutes, or until sealed. Add the cinnamon stick and ground cumin and cook, stirring constantly, for a further 2 minutes.

Add the carrots and sweet potato, then add the saffron with the soaking liquid and the stock. Bring to the boil, season to taste with salt and pepper, then reduce the heat to a simmer. Cover with a lid and simmer for 45 minutes, stirring occasionally.

Add the dates and continue to simmer for a further 15 minutes. Remove the cinnamon stick, adjust the seasoning and serve with freshly prepared couscous.

Chickpea Chorizo Stew

Serves 2

2 tbsp Spanish olive oil
2 chorizo sausages, sliced
1 Spanish onion, peeled
and chopped
1 green pepper, deseeded
and chopped
3 garlic cloves, peeled and
finely chopped
1/2 tsp dried marjoram
400 g can chickpeas, rinsed
and drained
4 tsp sun-dried tomato paste
125 ml/4 fl oz Spanish dry
white wine
600 ml/1 pint chicken stock
sea salt and freshly ground
black pepper
25 g/1 oz fresh white breadcrumbs
freshly chopped flat-leaf parsley,
to garnish
crusty bread, to serve

Heat the oil in a casserole dish or large, deep frying pan over a medium-high heat. Add the chorizo and cook, turning, for 2–3 minutes until starting to crisp. Remove and drain on absorbent kitchen paper. Drain the excess oil and fat, leaving 2 tbsp in the pan.

Return the pan to a medium heat. Add the onion and green pepper and cook, stirring, for 5 minutes, or until softened. Return the chorizo to the pan with the garlic and marjoram. Stir for a further minute, then add the chickpeas and tomato paste blended with 2 tablespoons water.

Pour in the wine and stock. Season with salt and pepper, then add the breadcrumbs, stir and bring to the boil. Reduce the heat to low and cook for a further 10 minutes, or until the sauce has thickened.

Garnish with chopped parsley and serve with crusty bread.

Oven-baked Pork Balls with Peppers

Serves 4

For the garlic bread:

2–4 garlic cloves, peeled
50 g/2 oz butter, softened
1 tbsp freshly chopped parsley
2–3 tsp lemon juice
1 focaccia loaf

For the pork balls:

450 g/1 lb fresh pork mince
4 tbsp freshly chopped basil
2 garlic cloves, peeled and chopped
3 sun-dried tomatoes, chopped
salt and freshly ground black pepper
3 tbsp olive oil
1 medium red pepper, deseeded and cut into chunks
1 medium green pepper, deseeded and cut into chunks
1 medium yellow pepper, deseeded and cut into chunks
225 g/8 oz cherry tomatoes
2 tbsp balsamic vinegar

Preheat oven to 200°C/400°F/Gas Mark 6, 15 minutes before cooking. Crush the garlic, then blend with the softened butter, the parsley and enough lemon juice to give a soft consistency. Shape into a roll, wrap in baking parchment paper and chill in the refrigerator for at least 30 minutes.

Mix together the pork, basil, 1 chopped garlic clove, sun-dried tomatoes and seasoning until well combined. With damp hands, divide the mixture into 16, roll into balls and reserve.

Spoon the olive oil in a large roasting tin and place in the preheated oven for about 3 minutes, until very hot. Remove from the heat and stir in the pork balls, the remaining chopped garlic and peppers. Bake for about 15 minutes. Remove from the oven and stir in the cherry tomatoes and season to taste with plenty of salt and pepper. Bake for about a further 20 minutes.

Just before the pork balls are ready, slice the bread, toast lightly and spread with the prepared garlic butter. Remove the pork balls from the oven, stir in the vinegar and serve immediately with garlic bread.

Spanish-style Pork Stew with Saffron Rice

Serves 4

2 tbsp olive oil
900 g/2 lb boneless
pork shoulder, diced
1 large onion, peeled and sliced
2 garlic cloves, peeled and
finely chopped
1 tbsp plain flour
450 g/1 lb plum tomatoes, peeled
and chopped
175 ml/6 fl oz red wine
1 tbsp freshly chopped basil
1 green pepper, deseeded and sliced
50 g/2 oz pimiento-stuffed olives,
cut in half crossways
salt and freshly ground black pepper
fresh basil leaves, to garnish

For the saffron rice:

1 tbsp olive oil, 25 g/1 oz butter,
1 small onion, peeled and
finely chopped,
few strands saffron, crushed
250 g/9 oz long-grain white rice
600 ml/1 pint chicken stock

Preheat the oven to 150°C/300°F/Gas Mark 2. Heat the oil in a large flameproof casserole and add the pork in batches. Fry over a high heat until browned. Transfer to a plate until all the pork is browned.

Lower the heat and add the onion to the casserole. Cook for a further 5 minutes until soft and starting to brown. Add the garlic and stir briefly before returning the pork to the casserole. Add the flour and stir.

Add the tomatoes. Gradually stir in the red wine and add the basil. Bring to simmering point and cover. Transfer the casserole to the lower part of the preheated oven and cook for 1¹/₂ hours. Stir in the green pepper and olives and cook for 30 minutes. Season to taste with salt and pepper.

Meanwhile, to make the saffron rice, heat the oil with the butter in a saucepan. Add the onion and cook for 5 minutes over a medium heat until softened. Add the saffron and rice and stir well. Add the stock, bring to the boil, cover and reduce the heat as low as possible. Cook for 15 minutes, covered, until the rice is tender and the stock is absorbed. Adjust the seasoning and serve with the stew, garnished with fresh basil.

Pastitsio (Greece)

Serves 4

butter, for greasing
2 tbsp olive oil
1 medium onion, peeled and chopped
2 celery stalks, trimmed and chopped
2 garlic cloves, peeled and chopped
450 g/1 lb lean minced beef or lamb
400 g/14 oz can chopped tomatoes
125 ml/4 fl oz red wine
1 tbsp tomato purée
1 cinnamon stick
1 tbsp dried oregano
2 tbsp chopped flat-leaf parsley
1 bay leaf
225 g/8 oz tubular pasta, such as
tortiglioni or large macaroni
mixed salad, to serve

For the topping:
300 ml/$^{1}/_{2}$ pint Greek yogurt
2 medium eggs
grated nutmeg, to taste
4 tbsp grated Greek kefalotiri hard
cheese or Parmesan cheese
15 g/$^{1}/_{2}$ oz white breadcrumbs

Preheat the oven to 190°C/350°F/Gas Mark 5, 10 minutes before using.

Grease a large baking tin, about 25 x 18 x 7.5 cm/10 x 7 x 3 inches with butter. Heat the oil in a large pan and fry the onion and celery until softened, add the garlic and fry for a further minute.

Add the minced meat and cook over a medium heat until browned. Add the chopped tomatoes, red wine, tomato purée, cinnamon and herbs and cook for a further 30 minutes, stirring occasionally, until thickened. Remove the cinnamon stick and bay leaf.

Meanwhile, cook the pasta in a large pan of boiling water for about 12 minutes until *al dente* then drain well. Make the topping by beating together the yogurt and eggs, then season with salt, black pepper and a few gratings of nutmeg.

Spread half the cooked pasta in the base of the prepared tin, cover with the meat mixture then with the remaining pasta. Pour over the yogurt mixture then sprinkle over the cheese and breadcrumbs. Bake in the oven for about 25 minutes until the top is golden brown. Serve with a mixed salad.

Stifado (Greece)

Serves 4

2 tbsp olive oil
900 g/2 lb braising steak, cubed
1 large onion, peeled and sliced
2 garlic cloves, peeled and chopped
3 tbsp tomato purée
300 ml/1/2 pint beef stock
175 ml/6 fl oz red wine
2 tbsp red wine vinegar
1 tsp caster sugar
1/2 tsp cloves
1/2 tsp cumin seeds
1 bay leaf
1 cinnamon stick
3 rosemary sprigs
salt and freshly ground black pepper
350 g/12 oz small onions, unpeeled
1–2 tbsp water (optional)

To serve:

sliced sautéed potatoes
Greek salad of tomatoes, cucumber,
sliced peppers, olives and cubes
of feta cheese

Preheat the oven to 170˚C/325˚F/Gas Mark 3, 15 minutes before using.

Heat half the oil in a large pan and fry the braising steak over a medium heat until it is browned on all sides. Lift the meat out with a slotted spoon and place it in a large flameproof casserole.

Heat the remaining oil in the same pan and fry the sliced onion until transparent. Stir in the garlic and cook for 1 minute, then stir in the tomato purée, stock, wine, vinegar and sugar. Bring to a simmer then pour into the casserole with the meat. Tie the cloves, cumin seeds, bay leaf, cinnamon stick and 2 sprigs of rosemary in a piece of muslin and add to the casserole.

Season well with salt and pepper, then cover the dish and cook for 1 1/2 hours.

Place the small onions in a pan of boiling water for a minute then drain and peel the skins away. Add the onions to the casserole dish and add the water if the meat is becoming dry. Cook for a further hour until the meat is very tender.

Serve garnished with the remaining rosemary sprig with sliced sautéed potatoes and a Greek salad of tomatoes, cucumber, sliced peppers, olives and cubes of feta cheese.

Lemon Chicken with Potatoes, Rosemary ❧ Olives

Serves 6

12 skinless boneless chicken thighs
1 large lemon
125 ml/4 fl oz extra-virgin olive oil
6 garlic cloves, peeled and sliced
2 onions, peeled and thinly sliced
bunch of fresh rosemary
1.1 kg/2^{1}/$_{2}$ lb potatoes, peeled and
cut into 4 cm/1^{1}/$_{2}$ inch pieces
salt and freshly ground black pepper
18–24 black olives, pitted

To serve:

steamed carrots
courgettes

Preheat oven to 200°C/ 400°F/Gas Mark 6, 15 minutes before cooking. Trim the chicken thighs and place in a shallow baking dish large enough to hold them in a single layer. Remove the rind from the lemon with a zester or, if using a peeler, cut into thin julienne strips. Reserve half and add the remainder to the chicken. Squeeze the lemon juice over the chicken, toss to coat well and leave to stand for 10 minutes.

Add the remaining lemon zest or julienne strips, olive oil, garlic, onions and half of the rosemary sprigs. Toss gently and leave for about 20 minutes.

Cover the potatoes with lightly salted water and bring to the boil. Cook for 2 minutes, then drain well and add to the chicken. Season to taste with salt and pepper.

Roast the chicken in the preheated oven for 50 minutes, turning frequently and basting, or until the chicken is cooked. Just before the end of cooking time, discard the rosemary, and add fresh sprigs of rosemary. Add the olives and stir. Serve immediately with steamed carrots and courgettes.

Chicken Chasseur

Serves 4

1 whole chicken, about 1.5 kg/3 lb
in weight, jointed into 4 or 8 portions
1 tbsp olive oil
1 tbsp unsalted butter
12 baby onions, peeled
2–4 garlic cloves, peeled and sliced
2 celery stalks, trimmed and sliced
175 g/6 oz closed cup
mushrooms, wiped
2 tbsp plain flour
300 ml/^{1}/$_2$ pint dry white wine
2 tbsp tomato puree
450 ml/^{3}/$_4$ pint chicken stock
salt and freshly ground black pepper
few sprigs fresh tarragon
350 g/12 oz sweet potatoes, peeled
and cut into chunks
300 g/10 oz shelled fresh or frozen
broad beans
1 tbsp freshly chopped tarragon,
to garnish

Preheat the oven to 180°C/350°F/Gas Mark 4. Skin the chicken, if preferred, and rinse lightly. Pat dry on absorbent paper towels. Heat the oil and butter in an ovenproof casserole (or frying pan, if preferred), add the chicken portions and cook, in batches, until browned all over. Remove with a slotted spoon and reserve.

Add the onions, garlic and celery to the casserole and cook for 5 minutes, or until golden. Cut the mushrooms in half if large, then add to the casserole and cook for 2 minutes.

Sprinkle in the flour and cook for 2 minutes, then gradually stir in the wine. Blend the tomato puree with a little of the stock in a small bowl, then stir into the casserole together with the remaining stock. Bring to the boil, stirring constantly.

If a frying pan has been used, transfer everything to a casserole. Return the chicken to the casserole, season to taste and add a few tarragon sprigs.

Stir in the sweet potato, cover with a lid and cook in the oven for 30 minutes. Remove the casserole from the oven and add the broad beans. Return to the oven and cook for a further 15–20 minutes, or until the chicken and vegetables are cooked. Serve sprinkled with chopped tarragon.

Avgolemono (Egg-Lemon Soup)

Serves 6

1.5 kg/3 lb whole oven-ready chicken
about 2.25 litres/4 pints water
2 tbsp sunflower oil
1 onion, peeled and finely chopped
1 large carrot, peeled and
roughly chopped
1 large leek, trimmed
2 bay leaves
175 g/6 oz arborio rice
2 medium eggs
4 tbsp freshly squeezed lemon juice
salt and freshly ground black pepper
1 tbsp freshly chopped parsley

Cook's tip:

Take care when adding the egg
and lemon juice to the soup,
otherwise the egg may curdle.

Wipe the chicken cavity with a damp cloth or kitchen paper, then place in a large saucepan and cover with the water. Bring to the boil over a medium heat, then cover with a lid, reduce the heat and simmer for 1 hour, or until tender. Remove from the heat and leave to cool.

When the chicken is cool enough to handle, remove from the stock and take the chicken from the bones. Discard the skin and cut the meat into bite-size pieces. Reserve.

Heat the oil in a frying pan, add all the vegetables and fry for 10 minutes, stirring frequently, then add to the chicken stock in the saucepan together with the bay leaves and rice. Bring to the boil, then reduce the heat and simmer for a further 30 minutes, or until the rice is tender. Add the chicken to the saucepan.

Beat the eggs with the lemon juice and pour in about 150 ml/$\frac{1}{4}$ pint of the warm stock, stirring through. Add a further 150 ml/$\frac{1}{4}$ pint of the stock, then carefully pour this into the saucepan, stirring all the time. Season to taste with salt and pepper and serve garnished with the chopped parsley.

Cassoulet

Serves 4

1 tbsp olive oil
1 onion, peeled and chopped
2 celery stalks, trimmed
and chopped
175 g/6 oz carrots, peeled and sliced
2–3 garlic cloves, peeled
and crushed
350 g/12 oz pork belly (optional)
8 spicy thick sausages, such
as Toulouse
few fresh thyme sprigs
salt and freshly ground black pepper
2 x 400 g/14 oz cans cannellini
beans, drained and rinsed
600 ml/1 pint vegetable stock
75 g/3 oz fresh breadcrumbs
2 tbsp freshly chopped thyme

Preheat the oven to 180°C/350°F/Gas Mark 4. Heat the
oil in a large saucepan or ovenproof casserole, add the
onion, celery, carrot and garlic and sauté for 5 minutes.
Cut the pork, if using, into small pieces and cut the
sausages into chunks.

Add the meat to the vegetables and cook, stirring, until lightly
browned.

Add the thyme sprigs and season to taste with salt and
pepper. If a saucepan was used, transfer everything to an
ovenproof casserole.

Spoon the beans on top, then pour in the stock. Mix the
breadcrumbs with 1 tablespoon of the chopped thyme in a
small bowl and sprinkle on top of the beans. Cover with a lid
and cook in the oven for 40 minutes. Remove the lid and
cook for a further 15 minutes, or until the breadcrumbs are
crisp. Sprinkle with the remaining chopped thyme and serve.

Spanish Garlic Chicken

Serves 4

1 whole roasting chicken, 1.5 kg/3 lb,
cut into even-sized pieces
3 tbsp Spanish extra virgin olive oil
3–4 garlic cloves
300 ml/¹/₂ pint Spanish dry
white wine
sea salt
300 ml/¹/₂ pint chicken stock
few fresh herbs sprigs, such as
chives, to garnish

Preheat the oven to 180˚C/350˚F/Gas Mark 4.

Rub the chicken pieces with 1 tablespoon of the extra virgin olive oil and place in a casserole dish.

Place the garlic cloves, 125 ml/4 fl oz of the white wine and salt to taste in a food processor and blend. Add 125 ml/4 fl oz of the stock and blend again until thoroughly mixed. Pour over the chicken. Cover the chicken with the lid and put in the oven on the centre shelf. Cook for 15 minutes, then baste the chicken joints with the cooking liquor.

Re-cover with the lid and return to the oven and continue to cook for 15 minutes before basting again with the wine and stock. Continue to cook, uncovered, for 30 minutes, basting with the wine and stock. Take care that the liquor does not evaporate completely.

After 30 minutes, check that the chicken is thoroughly cooked. Serve garnished with the herbs and with the liquor as a sauce.

Chicken with Roasted Fennel Citrus Rice

Serves 4

2 tsp fennel seeds
1 tbsp freshly chopped oregano
1 garlic clove, peeled and crushed
salt and freshly ground black pepper
4 chicken quarters, about
175 g/6 oz each
1/2 lemon, finely sliced
1 fennel bulb, trimmed
2 tsp olive oil
4 plum tomatoes
25 g/1 oz pitted green olives

To garnish:
fennel fronds
orange slices

For the citrus rice:
225 g/8 oz long-grain rice
finely grated zest and juice
of 1/2 lemon
150 ml/1/4 pint orange juice
450 ml/3/4 pint boiling chicken or
vegetable stock

Preheat the oven to 200°C/400°F/Gas Mark 6. Lightly crush the fennel seeds and mix with oregano, garlic, salt and pepper. Place between the skin and flesh of the chicken breasts, careful not to tear the skin. Arrange the lemon slices on top of the chicken.

Cut the fennel into eight wedges. Place on baking tray with the chicken. Lightly brush the fennel with the oil. Cook the chicken and fennel on the top shelf of the preheated oven for 10 minutes.

Meanwhile, put the rice in a 2.3 litre/4 pint ovenproof dish. Stir in the lemon zest and juice, orange juice and stock. Cover with a lid and put on the middle shelf of the oven. Reduce the oven temperature to 180°C/350°F/Gas Mark 4. Cook the chicken for a further 40 minutes, turning the fennel wedges and lemon slices once.

Deseed and chop the tomatoes. Add to the tray with the chicken and cook for 5–10 minutes. Remove from the oven.

When cooled slightly, remove the chicken skin and discard. Fluff the rice, scatter olives over the dish.

Garnish with fennel fronds and orange slices and serve.

Spicy Chicken Skewers with Mango Tabbouleh

Serves 4

400 g/14 oz chicken breast fillet
200 ml/7 fl oz natural/plain yogurt
1 garlic clove, peeled and crushed
1 small red chilli, deseeded and
finely chopped
1/2 tsp ground turmeric
finely grated zest and juice
of 1/2 lemon
fresh mint sprigs, to garnish

For the mango tabbouleh:

175 g/6 oz bulgur wheat
1 tsp olive oil
juice of 1/2 lemon
1/2 red onion, finely chopped
1 ripe mango, halved, stoned,
peeled and chopped
1/4 cucumber, finely diced
2 tbsp freshly chopped parsley
2 tbsp freshly shredded mint
salt and finely ground
black pepper

If using wooden skewers, pre-soak them in cold water for at least 30 minutes (this stops them from burning during grilling). Cut the chicken into 5 x 1 cm/2 x 1/2 inch strips and place in a shallow dish.

Mix together the yogurt, garlic, chilli, turmeric, lemon zest and juice. Pour over the chicken and toss to coat. Cover and leave to marinate in the refrigerator for up to 8 hours.

To make the tabbouleh, put the bulgur wheat in a bowl. Pour over enough boiling water to cover. Put a plate over the bowl. Leave to soak for 20 minutes. Whisk together the oil and lemon juice in a bowl. Add the red onion and leave to marinate for 10 minutes.

Drain the bulgur wheat and squeeze out any excess moisture in a clean dishtowel. Add to the red onion with the mango, cucumber and herbs and season to taste with salt and pepper. Toss together.

Thread the chicken strips onto eight wooden or metal skewers. Cook under a hot grill for 8 minutes. Turn and brush with the marinade, until the chicken is lightly browned and cooked through. Spoon the tabbouleh onto individual plates. Arrange the chicken skewers on top and garnish with the mint sprigs. Serve warm or cold.

Fish  Seafood

Many countries that border the Mediterranean Sea will have their own version of the recipes shown here – those that the sea itself provides them with. Fresh seafood is unsurprisingly at the heart of many Mediterranean cuisines – and is one of the reasons for the well-known health benefits assigned to the 'Mediterranean diet'. From unadorned Ratatouille Mackerel to deliciously flavoured fish stew, there's a whole world from which to choose.

Bouillabaisse (France)

Serves 4–6

675 g/1 1/2 lb assorted fish, such as
whiting, mackerel, red mullet,
salmon and king prawns, cleaned
and skinned
few saffron strands
3 tbsp olive oil
2 onions, peeled and sliced
2 celery stalks, trimmed and sliced
225 g/8 oz ripe tomatoes, peeled
and chopped
1 fresh bay leaf
2–3 garlic cloves, peeled
and crushed
1 bouquet garni
sea salt and freshly ground
black pepper
French bread, to serve

Cut the fish into thick pieces, peel the prawns if necessary and rinse well. Place the saffron strands in a small bowl, cover with warm water and leave to infuse for at least 10 minutes.

Heat the oil in a large heavy-based saucepan or casserole, add the onions and celery and fry for 5 minutes, stirring occasionally. Add the tomatoes, bay leaf, garlic and bouquet garni and stir until lightly coated with the oil.

Place the firm fish on top of the tomatoes and pour in the saffron-infused water and enough water to just cover. Bring to the boil, reduce the heat, cover with a lid and cook for 8 minutes.

Add the soft-flesh fish and continue to simmer for 5 minutes, or until all the fish are cooked. Season to taste with salt and pepper, remove and discard the bouquet garni and serve with French bread.

Sardines in Vine Leaves

Serves 4

8–16 vine leaves in brine, drained
2 spring onions
6 tbsp olive oil
2 tbsp lime juice
2 tbsp freshly chopped oregano
1 tsp mustard powder
salt and freshly ground black pepper
8 sardines, cleaned
8 bay leaves
8 sprigs of fresh dill

To garnish:

lime wedges
sprigs of fresh dill

To serve:

olive salad
crusty bread

Preheat the grill and line the grill rack with tinfoil just before cooking. Cut 8 pieces of string about 25.5 cm/10 inches long, and leave to soak in cold water for about 10 minutes. Cover the vine leaves in almost boiling water. Leave for 20 minutes, then drain and rinse thoroughly. Pat the vine leaves dry with absorbent kitchen paper.

Trim the spring onions and finely chop, then place into a small bowl. With a balloon whisk beat in the olive oil, lime juice, oregano, mustard powder and season to taste with salt and pepper. Cover with clingfilm and leave in the refrigerator, until required. Stir the mixture before using.

Prepare the sardines, by making 2 slashes on both sides of each fish and brush with a little of the lime juice mixture. Place a bay leaf and a dill sprig inside each sardine cavity and wrap with 1–2 vine leaves, depending on size. Brush with the lime mixture and tie the vine leaves in place with string.

Grill the fish for 4–5 minutes on each side under a medium heat, brushing with a little more of the lime mixture if necessary. Leave the fish to rest, unwrap and discard the vine leaves. Garnish with lime wedges and sprigs of fresh dill and serve with the remaining lime mixture, olive salad and crusty bread.

Catalan Fish Stew

Serves 4

225 g/8 oz large raw prawns
225 g/8 oz fresh clams
450 g/1 lb fresh mussels
6 tbsp Spanish olive oil
1 Spanish onion, peeled
and chopped
1 fennel bulb, trimmed
and chopped
1 red chilli, trimmed and chopped
2 garlic cloves, peeled
and chopped
few saffron strands
2 fresh bay leaves
300 ml/½ pint fish stock
150 ml/¼ pint Spanish white wine
salt and freshly ground
black pepper
450 g/1 lb firm white fish
flat-leaf parsley, to garnish

Clean the prawns and leave whole. Clean the clams and mussels, discarding any that are open. Keep in cold water until required.

Heat the oil in a large pan and fry the vegetables together with the chilli and garlic for 5 minutes. Add the saffron and bay leaves and fry for a further 2 minutes.

Add the stock and wine with seasoning to taste.

Skin the fish if necessary and remove any bones. Add to the stew together with the reserved prawns, mussels and clams. Bring to the boil. Cover with the lid and reduce the heat to a simmer.

Cook gently for 10–12 minutes until the fish and vegetables are tender. Discard any unopened mussels or clams. Serve garnished with flat-leaf parsley.

Ratatouille Mackerel

Serves 4

1 red pepper
1 white or red onion, peeled
1 tbsp olive oil
1 garlic clove, peeled and
thinly sliced
2 courgettes, trimmed and cut into
thick slices
400 g/14 oz can chopped tomatoes
sea salt and freshly ground
black pepper
4 x 275 g/10 oz small mackerel,
cleaned and heads removed
spray of olive oil
lemon juice, for drizzling
12 fresh basil leaves
couscous or rice mixed with
chopped parsley, to serve

Preheat the oven to 190°C/375°F/Gas Mark 5. Cut the top off the red pepper, remove the seeds and membrane, then cut into chunks. Cut the red onion into thick wedges.

Heat the oil in a large pan and cook the onion and garlic for 5 minutes, or until beginning to soften.

Add the pepper chunks and courgette slices and cook for a further 5 minutes.

Pour in the chopped tomatoes with their juice and cook for a further 5 minutes. Season to taste with salt and pepper and pour into an ovenproof dish.

Season the fish with salt and pepper and arrange on top of the vegetables. Spray with a little olive oil and lemon juice. Cover and cook in the preheated oven for 20 minutes.

Remove the cover, add the basil leaves and return to the oven for a further 5 minutes. Serve immediately with couscous or rice mixed with parsley.

Roasted Cod with Saffron Aïoli

Serves 4

For the saffron aïoli:

2 garlic cloves, peeled
¼ tsp saffron strands
sea salt, to taste
1 medium egg yolk
200 ml/7 fl oz extra-virgin olive oil
2 tbsp lemon juice

For the marinade:

2 tbsp olive oil
4 garlic cloves, peeled and
finely chopped
1 red onion, peeled and
finely chopped
1 tbsp freshly chopped rosemary
2 tbsp freshly chopped thyme
4–6 sprigs of fresh rosemary
1 lemon, sliced
4 x 175 g/6 oz thick cod fillets
with skin
freshly cooked vegetables, to serve

Preheat oven to 180°C/ 350°F/Gas Mark 4, 10 minutes before cooking. Crush the garlic, saffron and a pinch of salt in a pestle and mortar to form a paste. Place in a blender with the egg yolk and blend for 30 seconds. With the motor running, slowly add the olive oil in a thin, steady stream until the mayonnaise is smooth and thick. Spoon into a small bowl and stir in the lemon juice. Cover and leave in the refrigerator until required.

Combine the olive oil, garlic, red onion, rosemary and thyme for the marinade and leave to infuse for about 10 minutes.

Place the sprigs of rosemary and slices of lemon in the bottom of a lightly oiled roasting tin. Add the cod, skinned-side up. Pour over the prepared marinade and leave to marinate in the refrigerator for 15–20 minutes.

Bake in the preheated oven for 15–20 minutes, or until the cod is cooked and the flesh flakes easily with a fork. Leave the cod to rest for 1 minute before serving with the saffron aïoli and vegetables.

Cod with Fennel Cardamom

Serves 4

1 garlic clove, peeled and crushed
finely grated zest of 1 lemon
1 tsp lemon juice
1 tbsp olive oil
1 fennel bulb
1 tbsp cardamom pods
salt and freshly ground
black pepper
4 x 175 g/6 oz thick cod fillets

Preheat the oven to 190˚C/375˚F/Gas Mark 5. Place the garlic in a small bowl with the lemon zest, juice and olive oil and stir well.

Cover and leave to infuse for at least 30 minutes. Stir well before using.

Trim the fennel bulb, slice thinly and place in a bowl. Place the cardamom pods in a pestle and mortar and pound lightly to crack the pods. Alternatively, place in a polythene bag and pound gently with a rolling pin. Add the crushed cardamom to the fennel slices.

Season the fish with salt and pepper. Place onto four separate 20.5 x 20.5 cm/8 x 8 inch squares of baking parchment.

Spoon the fennel mixture over the fish and drizzle with the infused oil. Then fold the baking parchment over to enclose the fish and form a pocket. Place the pockets on a baking sheet and bake in the preheated oven for 8–10 minutes, or until cooked. Serve immediately in the paper pockets.

Spanish Omelette with Smoked Cod

Serves 3–4

3 tbsp sunflower oil
3 potatoes, peeled and diced
2 onions, peeled and cut
into wedges
2–4 large garlic cloves, peeled
and thinly sliced
1 large red pepper, deseeded,
quartered and thinly sliced
125 g/4¹/₂ oz smoked cod
salt and freshly ground black pepper
25 g/1 oz butter, melted
1 tbsp double cream
6 medium/large eggs, beaten
2 tbsp freshly chopped
flat-leaf parsley
50 g/2 oz grated mature
Cheddar cheese

To serve:

crusty bread
tossed green salad

Heat the oil in a large, nonstick, heavy-based frying pan, add the potatoes, onions and garlic and cook gently for 10–15 minutes until golden brown, then add the red pepper and cook for 3 minutes.

Meanwhile, place the fish in a shallow frying pan and cover with water. Season to taste with salt and pepper and poach gently for 10 minutes. Drain and flake the fish into a bowl, pour in the melted butter and cream, adjust the seasoning and reserve.

When the vegetables are cooked, drain off any excess oil and stir in the beaten eggs and parsley. Pour the fish mixture over the top and cook gently for 5 minutes, or until the eggs become firm.

Sprinkle the grated cheese over the top and place the pan under a preheated hot grill. Cook for 2–3 minutes until the cheese is golden and bubbling. Carefully slide the omelette onto a large plate and serve immediately with plenty of bread and salad.

Mussels Linguine

Serves 4

2 kg/4$^{1}/_{2}$ lb fresh mussels, washed
and scrubbed
knob butter
1 onion, peeled and finely chopped
300 ml/$^{1}/_{2}$ pint medium dry white wine

For the sauce:

1 tbsp sunflower oil
4 baby onions, peeled
and quartered
2 garlic cloves, peeled and crushed
400 g/14 oz can chopped tomatoes
large pinch salt
225 g/8 oz dried linguine
or tagliatelle
2 tbsp freshly chopped parsley

Soak the mussels in plenty of cold water. Leave in the refrigerator until required. When ready to use, scrub the mussel shells, removing any barnacles or beards. Discard any open mussels.

Melt the butter in a large pan. Add the mussels, onion and wine. Cover with a close-fitting lid and steam for 5–6 minutes, shaking the pan gently to ensure even cooking. Discard any mussels that have not opened, then strain and reserve the liquor.

To make the sauce, heat the oil in a medium-sized saucepan and gently fry the quartered onion and garlic for 3–4 minutes until soft and transparent. Stir in the tomatoes and half the reserved mussel liquor. Bring to the boil and simmer for 7–10 minutes until the sauce begins to thicken.

Cook the pasta in boiling salted water for 7 minutes or until *al dente*. Drain the pasta, reserving 2 tablespoons of the cooking liquor, then return the pasta and liquor to the pan.

Remove the meat from half the mussel shells. Stir into the sauce along with the remaining mussels. Pour the hot sauce over the cooked pasta and toss gently. Garnish with the parsley and serve immediately.

Paella (Spain)

Serves 6

450 g/1 lb live mussels
4 tbsp olive oil
6 medium-sized chicken thighs
1 onion, peeled and
finely chopped
1 garlic clove, peeled and crushed
225 g/8 oz tomatoes, skinned,
deseeded and chopped
1 red and 1 green pepper, deseeded
and chopped
125 g/4^1/$_2$ oz frozen peas
1 tsp paprika
450 g/1 lb Arborio rice
^{1}/$_2$ tsp turmeric
900 ml/1^1/$_2$ pints chicken stock,
warmed
175 g/6 oz large peeled prawns
salt and freshly ground black pepper
2 limes
1 lemon
1 tbsp freshly chopped basil
whole cooked unpeeled prawns,
to garnish

Rinse the mussels under cold running water, scrubbing well to remove any grit and barnacles, then pull off the hairy 'beards'. Tap any open mussels sharply with a knife, and discard if they refuse to close. Heat the oil in a paella pan or large heavy-based frying pan and cook the chicken thighs for 10–15 minutes until golden. Remove and keep warm.

Fry the onion and garlic in the remaining oil in the pan for 2–3 minutes, then add the tomatoes, peppers, peas and paprika and cook for a further 3 minutes. Add the rice to the pan and return the chicken with the turmeric and half the stock. Bring to the boil and simmer, gradually adding more stock as it is absorbed. Cook for 20 minutes, or until most of the stock has been absorbed and the rice is almost tender.

Put the mussels in a large saucepan with 5 cm/2 inches boiling salted water. Cover and steam for 5 minutes. Discard any with shells that have not opened, then stir into the rice with the prawns. Season to taste with salt and pepper. Heat through for 2–3 minutes until piping hot. Squeeze the juice from one of the limes over the paella. Cut the remaining lime and the lemon into wedges, arrange on top of the paella. Sprinkle with basil, garnish with prawns and serve.

Potato Boulangere with Sea Bass

Serves 2

450 g/1 lb potatoes, peeled and
thinly sliced
1 large onion, peeled and
thinly sliced
salt and freshly ground
black pepper
300 ml/¹/₂ pint fish or vegetable stock
75 g/3 oz butter or margarine
350 g/12 oz sea bass fillets
fresh flat-leaf parsley sprigs,
to garnish

Preheat the oven to 200°C/400°F/Gas Mark 6. Lightly grease a shallow 1.4 litre/2¹/₂ pint baking dish with oil or butter. Layer the potato slices and onions alternately in the prepared dish, seasoning each layer with salt and pepper.

Pour the stock over the top, then cut 50 g/2 oz/4 tbsp of the butter or margarine into small pieces and dot over the top layer. Bake in the preheated oven for 50–60 minutes. Do not cover the dish at this stage.

Lightly rinse the sea bass fillets and pat dry on absorbent paper towels. Cook in a griddle, or heat the remaining butter or margarine in a frying pan and shallow fry the fish fillets for 3–4 minutes per side, flesh side first. Remove from the pan with a slotted spatula and drain on absorbent paper towels.

Remove the partly cooked potato and onion mixture from the oven and place the fish on the top. Cover with kitchen foil and return to the oven for 10 minutes until heated through. Garnish with sprigs of parsley and serve immediately.

Seafood Risotto

Serves 4

50 g/2 oz butter
2 shallots, peeled and finely chopped
1 garlic clove, peeled and crushed
350 g/12 oz Arborio/risotto rice
150 ml/¹/₄ pint white wine
600 ml/1 pint fish or vegetable
stock, heated
125 g/4¹/₂ oz large prawns
50 g/2 oz smoked salmon trimmings
290 g/10 oz can baby clams
2 tbsp freshly chopped parsley
freshly grated Parmesan cheese,
to serve

To serve:

green salad
crusty bread

Melt the butter in a large heavy-based saucepan, add the shallots and garlic and cook for 2 minutes until slightly softened. Add the rice and cook for 1–2 minutes, stirring continuously, then pour in the wine and boil for 1 minute.

Pour in half the hot stock, bring to the boil, cover the saucepan and simmer gently for 15 minutes, adding the remaining stock a little at a time. Continue to simmer for 5 minutes, or until the rice is cooked and all the liquid is absorbed.

Meanwhile, prepare the fish by peeling the prawns and removing the headers and tails. Drain the clams and discard the liquid. Cut the smoked salmon trimmings into thin strips.

When the rice has cooked, stir in the prawns, smoked salmon strips, clams and half the chopped parsley, then heat through for 1–2 minutes until everything is piping hot. Turn into a serving dish, sprinkle with the remaining parsley and the Parmesan cheese and serve immediately with a green salad and crusty bread.

Seared Tuna with Pernod Thyme

Serves 4

4 tuna or swordfish steaks
salt and freshly ground
black pepper
3 tbsp Pernod
1 tbsp olive oil
zest and juice of 1 lime
2 tsp fresh thyme leaves
4 sun-dried tomatoes

To serve:

freshly cooked mixed rice
tossed green salad

Wipe the fish steaks with a damp cloth or dampened paper towels. Season both sides of the fish to taste with salt and pepper, then place in a shallow bowl and reserve.

Mix together the Pernod, olive oil, lime zest and juice with the fresh thyme leaves.

Finely chop the sun-dried tomatoes and add to the Pernod mixture. Pour the Pernod mixture over the fish and chill in the refrigerator for about 2 hours, occasionally spooning the marinade over the fish.

Heat a griddle or heavy-based frying pan. Drain the fish, reserving the marinade. Cook the fish for 3–4 minutes on each side for a steak that is still slightly pink in the middle. Or, if liked, cook the fish for 1–2 minutes longer on each side if you prefer your fish cooked through.

Place the remaining marinade in a small saucepan and bring to the boil. Pour the marinade over the fish and serve immediately, with the mixed rice and salad.

Pasta Provençale

Serves 4

2 tbsp olive oil
1 garlic clove, peeled and crushed
1 onion, peeled and finely chopped
1 small fennel bulb, trimmed and
halved and thinly sliced
400 g can chopped tomatoes
1 rosemary sprig, plus extra sprig
to garnish
350 g/12 oz monkfish, skinned
2 tsp lemon juice
400 g/14 oz gnocchi pasta
50 g/2 oz pitted black olives
200 g can flageolet beans,
drained and rinsed
1 tbsp freshly chopped oregano,
plus sprig to garnish
salt and freshly ground black pepper

Heat the olive oil in a large saucepan, add the garlic and onion and cook gently for 5 minutes. Add the fennel and cook for a further 5 minutes. Stir in the chopped tomatoes and rosemary sprig. Half-cover the pan and simmer for 10 minutes.

Cut the monkfish into bite-sized pieces and sprinkle with the lemon juice. Add to the tomatoes, cover and simmer gently for 5 minutes, or until the fish is opaque.

Meanwhile, bring a large pan of lightly salted water to a rolling boil. Add the pasta and cook according to the packet instructions, or until *al dente*. Drain the pasta thoroughly and return to the saucepan.

Remove the rosemary from the tomato sauce. Stir in the black olives, flageolet beans and chopped oregano, then season to taste with salt and pepper. Add the sauce to the pasta and toss gently together to coat, taking care not to break up the monkfish. Tip into a warmed serving bowl. Garnish with rosemary and oregano sprigs and serve immediately.

Red Pesto Clam Spaghetti

Serves 4

For the red pesto:
2 garlic cloves, peeled and finely chopped
50 g/2 oz pine nuts
25 g/1 oz fresh basil leaves
4 sun-dried tomatoes in oil, drained
4 tbsp olive oil
4 tbsp Parmesan cheese, grated
salt and freshly ground black pepper

For the clam sauce:
450 g/1 lb live clams, in their shells
1 tbsp olive oil
2 garlic cloves, peeled and crushed
1 small onion, peeled and chopped
5 tbsp medium dry white wine
150 ml/¼ pint fish or chicken stock
275 g/10 oz spaghetti

To make the red pesto, place the garlic, pine nuts, basil leaves, sun-dried tomatoes and olive oil in a food processor and blend in short, sharp bursts until smooth. Scrape into a bowl, then stir in the Parmesan cheese and season to taste with salt and pepper. Cover and leave in the refrigerator until required.

Scrub the clams with a soft brush and remove any beards from the shells, discard any shells that are open or damaged. Wash in plenty of cold water then leave in a bowl covered with cold water in the refrigerator until required. Change the water frequently.

Heat the olive oil in a large saucepan and gently fry the garlic and onion for 5 minutes until softened, but not coloured. Add the wine and stock and bring to the boil. Add the clams, cover and cook for 3–4 minutes, or until the clams have opened.

Discard any clams that have not opened and stir in the red pesto sauce. Bring a large saucepan of lightly salted water to the boil and cook the spaghetti for 5–7 minutes, or until *al dente*. Drain and return to the saucepan. Add the sauce to the spaghetti, mix well, then spoon into a serving dish and serve immediately.

Stuffed Squid with Romesco Sauce

Serves 4

8 small squid, about 350 g/12 oz
5 tbsp olive oil
50 g/2 oz pancetta, diced
1 onion, peeled and chopped
3 garlic cloves, peeled and finely chopped
2 tsp freshly chopped thyme
50 g/2 oz sun-dried tomatoes in oil drained, and chopped
75 g/3 oz fresh white breadcrumbs
2 tbsp freshly chopped basil
juice of $^1/_2$ lime
salt and freshly ground black pepper
2 vine-ripened tomatoes, peeled and finely chopped
pinch of dried chilli flakes
1 tsp dried oregano
1 large red pepper, skinned and chopped
assorted salad leaves, to serve

Preheat oven to 230°C/ 450°F/Gas Mark 8, 15 minutes before cooking. Clean the squid if necessary, rinse lightly, pat dry with absorbent kitchen paper and finely chop the tentacles.

Heat 2 tablespoons of the olive oil in a large non-stick frying pan and fry the pancetta for 5 minutes, or until crisp. Remove the pancetta and reserve. Add the tentacles, onion, 2 garlic cloves, thyme and sun-dried tomatoes to the oil remaining in the pan and cook gently for 5 minutes, or until softened. Remove the pan from the heat and stir in the diced pancetta. Blend in a food processor if a smoother stuffing is preferred, then stir in the breadcrumbs, basil and lime juice. Season to taste with salt and pepper and reserve. Spoon the stuffing into the cavity of the squid and secure the tops with cocktail sticks.

Place the squid in a large roasting tin, and sprinkle over 2 tablespoons each of oil and water. Place in the preheated oven and cook for 20 minutes.

Heat the remaining oil in a saucepan and cook the remaining garlic for 3 minutes. Add the tomatoes, chilli flakes and oregano and simmer gently for 15 minutes before stirring in the red pepper. Cook gently for a further 5 minutes. Blend in a food processor to make a smooth sauce and season to taste. Pour the sauce over the squid and serve immediately with some assorted salad leaves.

Mediterranean Fish Stew

Serves 4–6

4 tbsp olive oil
1 onion, peeled and finely sliced
5 garlic cloves, peeled and
finely sliced
1 fennel bulb, trimmed and
finely chopped
3 celery sticks, trimmed and
finely chopped
400 g can chopped tomatoes with
Italian herbs
1 tbsp freshly chopped oregano
1 bay leaf
zest and juice of 1 orange
1 tsp saffron strands
750 ml/1^1/$_4$ pints fish stock
3 tbsp dry vermouth
salt and freshly ground black pepper
225 g/8 oz thick haddock fillets
225 g/8 oz sea bass or bream fillets
225 g/8 oz raw tiger prawns, peeled
crusty bread, to serve

Heat the olive oil in a large saucepan. Add the onion, garlic, fennel and celery and cook over a low heat for 15 minutes, stirring frequently until the vegetables are soft and just beginning to turn brown.

Add the canned tomatoes with their juice, oregano, bay leaf, orange zest and juice with the saffron strands. Bring to the boil, then reduce the heat and simmer for 5 minutes. Add the fish stock, vermouth and season to taste with salt and pepper. Bring to the boil. Reduce the heat and simmer for 20 minutes.

Wipe or rinse the haddock and bass fillets and remove as many of the bones as possible. Place on a chopping board and cut into 5 cm/2 inch cubes. Add to the saucepan and cook for 3 minutes. Add the prawns and cook for a further 5 minutes. Adjust the seasoning to taste and serve with crusty bread.

Scallops Monkfish Kebabs with Fennel Sauce

Serves 4

700 g/1 1/2 lb monkfish tail
8 large fresh scallops
2 tbsp olive oil
1 garlic clove, peeled and crushed
freshly ground black pepper
1 fennel bulb, trimmed and
thinly sliced
assorted salad leaves, to serve

For the sauce:

2 tbsp fennel seeds
pinch of chilli flakes
4 tbsp olive oil
2 tsp lemon juice
salt and freshly ground
black pepper

Place the monkfish on a chopping board and remove the skin and the bone that runs down the centre of the tail and discard. Lightly rinse and pat dry with absorbent kitchen paper. Cut the fillets into 12 equal-sized pieces and place in a shallow bowl. Remove the scallops from their shells, if necessary, and clean thoroughly, discarding the black vein. Rinse lightly and pat dry. Put in the bowl. Blend the 2 tablespoons of olive oil, the crushed garlic and a pinch of black pepper in a small bowl, then pour the mixture over the fish, making sure they are well coated. Cover lightly and leave to marinate in the refrigerator for at least 30 minutes, or longer if time permits. Spoon over the marinade occasionally.

Lightly crush the fennel seeds and chilli flakes in a pestle and mortar. Stir in the 4 tablespoons of olive oil and lemon juice and season to taste with salt and pepper. Cover and leave to infuse for 20 minutes.

Drain the monkfish and scallops, reserving the marinade and thread on to 4 skewers. Spray a griddle pan with a fine spray of oil, then heat until almost smoking and cook the kebabs for 5–6 minutes, turning halfway through and brushing with the marinade throughout.

Brush the fennel slices with the fennel sauce and cook on the griddle for 1 minute on each side. Serve the fennel slices, topped with the kebabs and drizzled with the fennel sauce. Serve with assorted salad leaves.

Vegetables

All the countries in the Mediterranean region boast the freshness of sun-kissed vegetables due to the temperate climate they enjoy and thus the perfect growing conditions experienced. Freshly picked vegetables are bursting with vitamins, are cheap to buy and recipes can often be amended to ensure that the most seasonal ones are used. Vegetables are very versatile and can be used as starters, to accompany a main course, or can easily be a tasty meal in themselves.

Chunky Vegetable & Fennel Goulash with Dumplings

Serves 4

2 fennel bulbs, weighing about
450 g/1 lb
2 tbsp sunflower oil
1 large onion, peeled and sliced
1¹/₂ tbsp paprika
1 tbsp plain flour
300 ml/¹/₂ pint vegetable stock
400 g/14 oz can chopped tomatoes
450 g/1 lb potatoes, peeled and cut
into 2.5 cm/1 inch chunks
125 g/4 oz small button mushrooms
salt and freshly ground black pepper

For the dumplings:
1 tbsp sunflower oil
1 small onion, peeled and
finely chopped
1 egg
3 tbsp milk
3 tbsp freshly chopped parsley
125 g/4 oz fresh white breadcrumbs

Cut the fennel bulbs in half widthways. Thickly slice the stalks and cut the bulbs into 8 wedges. Heat the oil in a large saucepan or flameproof casserole. Add the onion and fennel and cook gently for 10 minutes until soft. Stir in the paprika and flour.

Remove from the heat and gradually stir in the stock. Add the chopped tomatoes, potatoes and mushrooms. Season to taste with salt and pepper. Bring to the boil, reduce the heat and simmer for 20 minutes.

Meanwhile, make the dumplings. Heat the oil in a frying pan and gently cook the onion for 10 minutes until soft. Leave to cool for a few minutes.

In a bowl, beat the egg and milk together, then add the onion, parsley and breadcrumbs and season to taste. With damp hands form the breadcrumb mixture into 12 round dumplings each about the size of a walnut.

Arrange the dumplings on top of the goulash. Cover and cook for a further 15 minutes, until the dumplings are cooked and the vegetables are tender. Serve immediately.

Imam Bayildi (Turkey)

Serves 4

4 aubergines
salt and freshly ground black pepper
150 ml/¹/₄ pint olive oil
2 medium onions, peeled and
thinly sliced
3 garlic cloves, peeled and
finely chopped
1 medium red chilli, deseeded
and chopped
4 ripe tomatoes, peeled and
chopped or 225 g/8 oz canned
chopped tomatoes
1 tsp harissa paste
250 ml/8 fl oz tomato juice
1 tsp caster sugar
1 tbsp lemon juice

To serve:

2 tbsp chopped flat-leaf parsley
cucumber and yogurt salad

Cut the aubergines in half lengthways, then scoop out half the pulp from the middle of each half, leaving a layer of flesh round the edges, being careful not to break the skins. Sprinkle the inside of each shell with salt and leave to drain, inverted in a colander for 30 minutes to allow the bitter juices to drain away. Rinse the shells under cold running water.

Heat 3 tbsp olive oil in a pan and fry the onions over a low heat for 10 minutes until softened. Add the garlic and chilli and fry for a further 5 minutes. Remove from the heat, add the chopped tomatoes and harissa paste.

Spoon the filling into the aubergine halves and arrange them side by side in a wide shallow pan.

Mix the tomato juice with the remaining olive oil, sugar, lemon juice, ¹/₂ tsp salt and freshly ground black pepper. Pour the mixture round the filled aubergine halves, cover and simmer gently for 30–40 minutes until soft and tender. Place two halves on a plate, spoon any juices from the pan over the aubergine halves, sprinkle with chopped parsley and serve with a fresh cucumber and yogurt salad.

Potato Gnocchi with Pesto Sauce

Serves 6

900 g/2 lb floury potatoes
40 g/1½ oz butter
1 egg, beaten
225 g/8 oz plain flour
1 tsp salt
freshly ground black pepper
25 g/1 oz shaved Parmesan cheese
rocket salad, to serve

For the pesto sauce:

50 g/2 oz fresh basil leaves
1 large garlic clove, peeled
2 tbsp pine nuts
120 ml/4 fl oz olive oil
40 g/1½ oz grated
Parmesan cheese

Cook the potatoes in their skins in boiling water for 20 minutes, or until tender. Drain and peel. While still warm, push the potatoes through a fine sieve into a bowl. Stir in the butter, egg, 175 g/6 oz of the flour and the salt and pepper.

Sift the remaining flour onto a board or work surface and add the potato mixture. Gently knead in enough flour until a soft, slightly sticky dough is formed. With floured hands, break off portions of the dough and roll into 2.5 cm/1 inch thick ropes. Cut into 2 cm/³/₄ inch lengths. Lightly press each piece against the inner prongs of a fork. Put on a tray covered with a floured dishtowel and chill in the refrigerator for about 30 minutes.

To make the pesto sauce, put the basil, garlic, pine nuts and oil in a processor and blend until smooth and creamy. Turn into a bowl and stir in the Parmesan cheese. Season to taste.

Cooking in several batches, drop the gnocchi into a saucepan of barely simmering salted water. Cook for 3–4 minutes, or until they float to the surface. Remove with a slotted spoon and keep warm in a covered oiled baking dish in a low oven. Add the gnocchi to the pesto sauce and toss gently to coat. Serve immediately, scattered with the Parmesan cheese and accompanied by a rocket salad.

Spanish Baked Tomatoes

Serves 4

175 g/6 oz wholegrain rice
600 ml/1 pint vegetable stock
2 tsp sunflower oil
2 shallots, peeled and
finely chopped
1 garlic clove, peeled and crushed
1 green pepper, deseeded and cut
into small cubes
1 red chilli, deseeded and
finely chopped
50 g/2 oz button mushrooms,
finely chopped
1 tbsp freshly chopped oregano
salt and freshly ground
black pepper
4 large ripe beef tomatoes
I large egg, beaten
1 tsp caster sugar
basil leaves, to garnish
crusty bread, to serve

Preheat the oven to 180°C/350°F/Gas Mark 4. Place the rice in a saucepan, pour over the vegetable stock and bring to the boil. Simmer for 30 minutes, or until the rice is tender. Drain and turn into a mixing bowl.

Add 1 teaspoon sunflower oil to a small nonstick frying pan and gently fry the shallots, garlic, pepper, chilli and mushrooms for 2 minutes. Add to the rice with the chopped oregano. Season with plenty of salt and pepper.

Slice the top off each tomato. Cut and scoop out the flesh, removing the hard core. Pass the tomato flesh through a sieve and add 1 tablespoon of the juice to the rice mixture. Stir in the beaten egg and mix. Sprinkle a little sugar in the base of each tomato, then pile the rice mixture into the shells.

Place the tomatoes in a baking dish and pour a little cold water around them. Replace their lids and drizzle a few drops of sunflower oil over the tops.

Bake in the preheated oven for about 25 minutes. Garnish with the basil leaves and season with black pepper and serve immediately with crusty bread.

Light Ratatouille

Serves 4

1 red pepper
2 courgettes, trimmed
1 small aubergine, trimmed
1 onion, peeled
2 ripe tomatoes
50 g/2 oz button mushrooms, wiped and halved or quartered
200 ml/7 fl oz tomato juice
1 tbsp freshly chopped basil
salt and freshly ground black pepper

Deseed the peppers, remove the membrane with a small sharp knife and cut into small dice. Thickly slice the courgettes and cut the aubergine into small dice. Slice the onion into rings.

Place the tomatoes in boiling water until their skins begin to peel away. Remove the skins, cut into quarters and remove the seeds.

Place all the vegetables, including the mushrooms, in a saucepan with the tomato juice and basil. Season to taste with salt and pepper. Bring to the boil, cover and simmer for 15 minutes, or until the vegetables are tender. Remove the vegetables with a slotted spoon and arrange in a serving dish.

Bring the liquid in the pan to the boil and boil for 20 seconds until it is slightly thickened. Season to taste with salt and pepper. Pass the sauce through a sieve to remove some of the seeds and pour over the vegetables. Serve the ratatouille hot or cold.

Rice-filled Peppers

Serves 4

8 ripe tomatoes
2 tbsp olive oil
1 onion, peeled and chopped
1 garlic clove, peeled and crushed
$^1/_2$ tsp dark muscovado sugar
125 g/4 oz cooked long-grain rice
50 g/2 oz pine nuts, toasted
1 tbsp freshly chopped oregano
salt and freshly ground black pepper
2 large red peppers
2 large yellow peppers

To serve:

mixed salad
crusty bread

Preheat oven to 200°C/ 400°F/Gas Mark 6. Put the tomatoes in a small bowl and pour over boiling water to cover. Leave for 1 minute, then drain. Plunge the tomatoes into cold water to cool, then peel off the skins. Quarter, remove the seeds and chop.

Heat the olive oil in a frying pan, and cook the onion gently for 10 minutes, until softened. Add the garlic, chopped tomatoes and sugar. Gently cook the tomato mixture for 10 minutes until thickened. Remove from the heat and stir the rice, pine nuts and oregano into the sauce. Season to taste with salt and pepper.

Halve the peppers lengthways, cutting through and leaving the stem on. Remove the seeds and cores, then put the peppers in a lightly oiled roasting tin, cut-side down and cook in the preheated oven for about 10 minutes.

Turn the peppers so they are cut side up. Spoon in the filling, then cover with tinfoil. Return to the oven for 15 minutes, or until the peppers are very tender, removing the tinfoil for the last 5 minutes to allow the tops to brown a little.

Serve 1 red pepper half and 1 yellow pepper half per person with a mixed salad and plenty of warmed, crusty bread.

Sicilian Baked Aubergine

Serves 4

1 large aubergine, trimmed
and cubed
2 celery stalks, trimmed
4 large ripe tomatoes
1 tsp sunflower oil
2 shallots, peeled and
finely chopped
1^{1}/$_{2}$ tsp tomato puree
5 large green pitted olives
5 large black pitted olives
salt and freshly ground
black pepper
1 tbsp white wine vinegar
2 tsp caster sugar
1 tbsp freshly chopped basil,
to garnish
mixed salad leaves, to serve

Preheat the oven to 200˚C/400˚F/Gas Mark 6. Place the aubergine on an oiled baking sheet. Cover the tray with kitchen foil and bake in the preheated oven for 15–20 minutes until soft. Remove the aubergine from the oven and leave to cool.

Place the celery and tomatoes in a large bowl and cover with boiling water. Remove the tomatoes from the bowl when their skins begin to peel away. Remove the skins, then deseed and chop the flesh into small pieces. Remove the celery from the bowl of water, chop finely and reserve.

Pour the sunflower oil into a nonstick saucepan, add the chopped shallots and fry gently for 2–3 minutes until soft. Add the celery, tomatoes, tomato puree and olives. Season to taste with salt and pepper. Simmer gently for 3–4 minutes.

Add the vinegar, sugar and cooled aubergine to the pan and heat gently for 2–3 minutes until all the ingredients are well blended. Remove from the heat and leave to cool, then garnish with the chopped basil and serve cold with salad leaves.

Three Bean Tagine (Morocco)

Serves 4

few saffron strands
2–3 tbsp olive oil
1 small aubergine, trimmed
and diced
1 onion, peeled and chopped
350 g/12 oz sweet potatoes,
peeled and diced
225 g/8 oz carrots, peeled
and chopped
1 cinnamon stick, bruised
1¹/₂ tsp ground cumin
salt and freshly ground black pepper
600 ml/1 pint vegetable stock
2 sprigs of fresh mint
200 g/7 oz can red kidney
beans, drained
300 g/10 oz can haricot
beans, drained
300 g/10 oz can flageolet
beans, drained
100 g/4 oz ready-to-eat dried
apricots, chopped
1 tbsp freshly chopped mint,
to garnish

Place warm water into a small bowl and sprinkle with saffron strands. Leave to infuse for at least 10 minutes.

Heat the oil in a large, heavy-based saucepan, add the aubergine and onion and sauté for 5 minutes before adding the sweet potato, carrots, cinnamon stick and ground cumin. Cook, stirring, until the vegetables are lightly coated in the cumin. Add the saffron with the soaking liquid and season to taste with salt and pepper. Pour in the stock and add the mint sprigs.

Rinse the beans, add to the pan and bring to the boil. Reduce the heat, cover with a lid and simmer for 20 minutes. Add the apricots and cook, stirring occasionally, for a further 10 minutes or until the vegetables are tender. Adjust the seasoning to taste, then serve sprinkled with chopped mint.

Vegetarian Cassoulet (France)

Serves 4

225 g/8 oz dried haricot beans,
soaked overnight
2 medium onions
1 bay leaf
1.4 litres/2^1/$_2$ pints cold water
550 g/1^1/$_4$ lb large potatoes, peeled
and cut into 1 cm/^{1}/$_2$ inch slices
5 tsp olive oil
1 large garlic clove,
peeled and crushed
2 leeks, trimmed and sliced
200 g/7 oz can chopped tomatoes
1 tsp muscovado sugar
1 tbsp freshly chopped thyme
2 tbsp freshly chopped parsley
salt and freshly ground
black pepper
3 courgettes, trimmed and sliced

For the topping:
50 g/2 oz fresh white breadcrumbs
25 g/1 oz Cheddar cheese,
finely grated

Preheat the oven to 180°C/350°F/Gas Mark 4, 10 minutes before required. Drain the beans, rinse under cold running water and put in a saucepan. Peel 1 of the onions and add to the beans with the bay leaf. Pour in the water. Bring to a rapid boil and cook for 10 minutes, then turn down the heat, cover and simmer for 50 minutes, or until the beans are almost tender. Drain the beans, reserving the liquor, but discarding the onion and bay leaf.

Cook the potatoes in a saucepan of lightly salted boiling water for 6–7 minutes until almost tender when tested with the point of a knife. Drain and reserve.

Peel and chop the remaining onion. Heat the oil in a frying pan and cook the onion with the garlic and leeks for 10 minutes until softened. Stir in the tomatoes, sugar, thyme and parsley. Stir in the beans, with 300 ml/^{1}/$_2$ pint of the reserved liquor and season to taste. Simmer, uncovered, for 5 minutes.

Layer the potato slices, courgettes and ladlefuls of the bean mixture in a large flameproof casserole. To make the topping, mix together the breadcrumbs and cheese and sprinkle over the top. Bake in the preheated oven for 40 minutes, or until the vegetables are cooked through and the topping is golden brown and crisp. Serve immediately.

Pasta with Courgettes, Rosemary & Lemon

Serves 4

350 g/12 oz dried pasta
shapes, such as rigatoni
1 1/2 tbsp good-quality extra virgin
olive oil
2 garlic cloves, peeled and
finely chopped
4 courgettes, thinly sliced
1 tbsp freshly chopped rosemary
1 tbsp freshly chopped parsley
zest and juice of 2 lemons
25 g/1 oz pitted black olives,
roughly chopped
25 g/1 oz pitted green olives,
roughly chopped
salt and freshly ground
black pepper

To garnish:

lemon slices
fresh rosemary sprigs

Bring a large saucepan of salted water to a rolling boil and add the pasta. Return to the boil and cook until *al dente*, or according to the packet instructions.

When the pasta is almost done, heat the oil in a large frying pan and add the garlic. Cook over a medium heat until the garlic just begins to brown. Be careful not to overcook the garlic at this stage or it will become bitter.

Add the courgettes, rosemary, parsley and lemon zest and juice. Cook for 3–4 minutes until the courgettes are just tender. Add the olives to the frying pan and stir well. Season to taste with salt and pepper and remove from the heat.

Drain the pasta well. Add to the frying pan. Stir until thoroughly combined. Garnish with lemon and fresh rosemary. Serve immediately.

Courgette Tarragon Tortilla

Serves 6

5–6 potatoes
3 tbsp olive oil
1 onion, peeled and thinly sliced
salt and freshly ground
black pepper
1 courgette, trimmed and
thinly sliced
6 eggs
2 tbsp freshly chopped tarragon
tomato wedges, to serve

Peel the potatoes and slice thinly. Dry the slices in a clean dishtowel to get them as dry as possible. Heat the oil in a large heavy-based pan, add the onion and cook for 3 minutes. Add the potatoes with a little salt and pepper, then stir the potatoes and onion lightly to coat in the oil.

Reduce the heat to the lowest possible setting, cover and cook gently for 5 minutes. Turn the potatoes and onion over and continue to cook for a further 5 minutes. Give the pan a shake every now and again to ensure that the potatoes do not stick to the base or burn. Add the courgette, then cover and cook for a further 10 minutes.

Beat the eggs and tarragon together and season to taste with salt and pepper. Pour the egg mixture over the vegetables and return to the heat. Cook on a low heat for up to 20–25 minutes, or until there is no liquid egg left on the surface of the tortilla.

Turn the tortilla over by inverting it onto a saucepan lid or a flat plate, then sliding it back into the pan. Return the pan to the heat and cook for a final 3–5 minutes, or until the underside is golden brown. If preferred, place the tortilla under a preheated grill for 4 minutes, or until set and golden brown on top. Cut into small squares and serve hot or cold with tomato wedges.

Tortellini, Cherry Tomato Mozzarella Skewers

Serves 6

250 g/9 oz mixed green and plain
cheese or vegetable-filled
fresh tortellini
150 ml/¹/₄ pint extra virgin olive oil
2 garlic cloves, peeled and crushed
pinch dried thyme or basil
salt and freshly ground
black pepper
225 g/8 oz cherry tomatoes
450 g/1 lb mozzarella, cut into
2.5 cm/1 inch cubes
basil leaves, to garnish
dressed salad leaves, to serve

Preheat the grill and line a grill pan with tinfoil, just before cooking. Bring a large pan of lightly salted water to a rolling boil. Add the tortellini and cook according to the packet instructions, or until *al dente*. Drain, rinse under cold running water, drain again and toss with 2 tablespoons of the olive oil and reserve.

Pour the remaining olive oil into a small bowl. Add the crushed garlic and thyme or basil, then blend well. Season to taste with salt and black pepper and reserve.

To assemble the skewers, thread the tortellini alternately with the cherry tomatoes and cubes of mozzarella. Arrange the skewers on the grill pan and brush generously on all sides with the olive oil mixture.

Cook the skewers under the preheated grill for about 5 minutes, or until they begin to turn golden, turning them halfway through cooking. Arrange 2 skewers on each plate and garnish with a few basil leaves. Serve immediately with dressed salad leaves.

Spinach, Pine Nut Mascarpone Pizza

Serves 2–4

For the basic pizza dough:
225 g/8 oz strong white/bread flour
1/2 tsp salt
1/4 tsp quick-acting dried yeast
150 ml/1/4 pint warm water
1 tbsp extra virgin olive oil

For the topping:
3 tbsp olive oil
1 large red onion, peeled
and chopped
2 garlic cloves, peeled and
finely sliced
450 g/1 lb frozen spinach, thawed
and drained
salt and freshly ground
black pepper
3 tbsp passata/tomato puree
125 g/4 oz mascarpone cheese
1 tbsp toasted pine nuts

Preheat the oven to 220°C/425°F/Gas Mark 7. Sift the flour and salt into a bowl and stir in the yeast. Make a well in the centre and gradually add the water and oil to form a soft dough. Knead the dough on a floured surface for about 5 minutes until smooth and elastic. Place in a lightly oiled bowl and cover with clingfilm. Leave to rise in a warm place for 1 hour.

Knock the pizza dough with your fist a few times, shape and roll out thinly on a lightly floured board. Place on a lightly floured baking sheet and lift the edge to make a little rim. Place another baking sheet into the preheated oven to heat up.

Heat half the oil in a frying pan and gently fry the onion and garlic until soft and starting to change colour.

Squeeze out any excess water from the spinach and chop finely. Add to the onion and garlic with the remaining olive oil. Season to taste with salt and pepper.

Spread the passata on the pizza dough and top with the spinach mixture. Mix the mascarpone with the pine nuts and dot over the pizza. Slide the pizza onto the hot baking sheet and bake for 15–20 minutes. Transfer to a large plate and serve immediately.

Vegetables Braised in Olive Oil Lemon

Serves 4

small strip of pared rind and juice
of ¹/₂ lemon
4 tbsp olive oil
1 bay leaf
large sprig of thyme
150 ml/¹/₄ pint water
4 spring onions, trimmed and
finely chopped
175 g/6 oz baby button mushrooms
175 g/6 oz broccoli, cut into
small florets
175 g/6 oz cauliflower, cut into
small florets
1 medium courgette, sliced on
the diagonal
2 tbsp freshly snipped chives
salt and freshly ground
black pepper
lemon zest, to garnish

Put the pared lemon rind and juice into a large saucepan. Add the olive oil, bay leaf, thyme and the water. Bring to the boil. Add the spring onions and mushrooms. Top with the broccoli and cauliflower, trying to add them so that the stalks are submerged in the water and the tops are just above it. Cover and simmer for 3 minutes.

Scatter the courgettes on top, so that they are steamed rather than boiled. Cook, covered, for a further 3–4 minutes, until all the vegetables are tender. Using a slotted spoon, transfer the vegetables from the liquid into a warmed serving dish. Increase the heat and boil rapidly for 3–4 minutes, or until the liquid is reduced to about 8 tablespoons. Remove the lemon rind, bay leaf and thyme sprig and discard.

Stir the chives into the reduced liquid, season to taste with salt and pepper and pour over the vegetables. Sprinkle with lemon zest and serve immediately.

Desserts

Despite the fact that most Mediterranean people are not great dessert eaters, what they do enjoy is eating locally grown fruits when they are in season, picked straight from the trees. In the wintertime, when fresh fruits are not so readily available, many of these recipes could easily be amended to incorporate dried fruits from the store cupboard and delicious cheese, nut and fruit combinations, not to mention chocolate!

Raspberry Soufflé

Serves 4

125 g/4¹/₂ oz redcurrants
50 g/2 oz sugar
1 sachet/3 tsp powdered gelatine
3 medium/large eggs, separated
300 g/¹/₂ pint Greek yogurt
450 g/1 lb raspberries, thawed
if frozen

To decorate:

mint sprigs
extra fruits

Wrap a band of double thickness greaseproof paper around the outside of four ramekin dishes. Make sure that 5 cm/2 inches of the paper stays above the top of each dish. Secure the paper to the dish with an elastic band or sticky tape.

Place the redcurrants and 1 tablespoon of the sugar in a small saucepan. Cook for 5 minutes until softened. Remove from the heat, press through a sieve and reserve.

Place 3 tablespoons water in a small bowl and sprinkle over the gelatine. Allow to stand for 5 minutes until spongy. Place the bowl over a pan of simmering water and leave until dissolved. Remove and allow to cool.

Beat together the remaining sugar and the egg yolks until thick, pale and creamy, then fold in the yogurt with a metal spoon or rubber spatula until well blended.

Press the raspberries through a sieve and fold into the yogurt mixture with the gelatine. Whisk the egg whites until stiff and fold into the yogurt mixture. Pour into the prepared dishes and chill in the refrigerator for 2 hours until firm.

Remove the paper from the dishes and spread the redcurrant puree over the top of the soufflés. Decorate with mint sprigs and extra fruits and serve.

Summer Fruit Semifreddo (Italy)

Serves 6–8

225 g/8 oz raspberries
125 g/4¹/₂ oz blueberries
125 g/4¹/₂ oz redcurrants
50 g/2 oz icing sugar
juice of 1 lemon
1 vanilla pod, split
50 g/2 oz sugar
4 large eggs, separated
600 ml/1 pint double cream
pinch salt
fresh redcurrants, to decorate

Wash and remove stalks from the fruits, as necessary, then put them into a food processor or blender with the icing sugar and lemon juice. Blend to a puree, pour into a jug and chill in the refrigerator until needed.

Remove the seeds from the vanilla pod by opening the pod and scraping with the back of a knife. Add the seeds to the sugar and whisk with the egg yolks until pale and thick.

In another bowl, whip the cream until soft peaks form. Do not overwhip. In a third bowl, whip the egg whites with the salt until stiff peaks form.

Using a large metal spoon (to avoid knocking any air from the mixture), fold together the fruit puree, egg yolk mixture, the cream and egg whites. Transfer the mixture to a round, shallow, lidded freezer box and put into the freezer until almost frozen. If the mixture freezes solid, thaw in the refrigerator until semi-frozen. Turn out the semi-frozen mixture, cut into wedges and serve decorated with a few fresh redcurrants. If the mixture thaws completely, eat immediately and do not re-freeze.

Crema Catalana

Serves 6

500 ml/18 fl oz double cream
1 tsp vanilla extract
125 g/4 oz caster sugar
6 medium egg yolks
6 heaped teaspoons
demerara sugar
sweet biscuits, to serve

Preheat the oven to 150°C/300°F/Gas Mark 2. Pour the cream into a heavy-based saucepan and add the vanilla extract. Place over a medium heat and bring to the boil. Reduce the heat to a simmer and cook for 5 minutes.

Meanwhile, beat the sugar and egg yolks together until pale and creamy. Return the cream to the boil then whisk into the egg and sugar. Continue to whisk until the mixture thickens.

Strain the mixture through a fine sieve and pour into 6 x 150 ml/ 1/4 pint ramekins or ovenproof dishes. Leave a space at the top where the sugar can be sprinkled.

Place the dishes in a roasting tin and carefully pour in boiling water to come halfway up the sides of the dishes. Take care while placing in the oven and cook for 35–40 minutes until the custard is set, but still has a wobble in the middle. Remove from the oven and cool, then place in the refrigerator to chill overnight.

When ready to serve, sprinkle with the demerara sugar and place under a preheated grill, turning as necessary until the sugar has lightly caramelized. Chill in the refrigerator for a few minutes, then serve with sweet biscuits.

Baklava (Greece and Turkey)

Makes about 38 squares

75 g/3 oz butter, melted, plus extra
for greasing
175 g/6 oz walnut pieces
175 g/6 oz almonds
75 g/3 oz caster sugar
1 tbsp ground cinnamon
$^1/_4$ tsp ground nutmeg
2 x 275 g/10 oz packs filo pastry

For the syrup and topping:

450 g/1 lb caster sugar
1 cinnamon stick
6 tbsp cold water
3 tbsp lemon juice
100 g/3$^1/_2$ oz shelled pistachio
nuts, finely chopped

Preheat the oven to 180˚C/350˚F/Gas Mark 4, 15 minutes before using. Brush a 33 x 23 cm/13 x 9 inch Swiss roll tin with melted butter.

Put the nuts, sugar and ground spices in a food processor fitted with a metal blade and blitz until finely chopped.

Carefully unfold the sheets of filo on a clean, dry work surface, keeping half the pastry covered with clingfilm to prevent it from drying out. Brushing each sheet with meted butter, line the tin with half the pastry sheets, overlapping the sheets and folding where necessary.

Spoon the nut mixture over the pastry and smooth level with a palette knife. Cover with the remaining pastry, layering and brushing between each sheet with melted butter. Using a sharp serrated knife, cut into squares about 4 cm/ 1$^3/_4$ inches wide. Bake for 30–35 minutes until pale golden and crisp.

Meanwhile, make the syrup. Put the sugar, cinnamon and cold water in a heavy-based pan and heat gently until the sugar has dissolved. Reduce the heat to low and simmer for 5 minutes to thicken. Remove from the heat and stir in the lemon juice. Pour the warm syrup over the baklava when it comes out of the oven, sprinkle over the chopped pistachio nuts, then leave to cool in the tray on a wire rack.

Crème Brûlée with Sugared Raspberries

Serves 4

600 ml/1 pint fresh whipping cream
4 medium/large egg yolks
75 g/3 oz caster sugar
1/2 tsp vanilla essence
25 g/1 oz/2 tbsp demerara/light
brown sugar
175 g/6 oz fresh raspberries

Preheat the oven to 150°C/300°F/Gas Mark 2. Pour the cream into a bowl and place over a saucepan of gently simmering water. Heat gently but do not allow to boil.

Meanwhile, whisk together the egg yolks, 50 g/2 oz of the caster sugar and the vanilla essence. When the cream is warm, pour it over the egg mixture, whisking briskly until it is mixed completely.

Pour into 6 individual ramekin dishes and place in a roasting tin. Fill the tin with sufficient water to come halfway up the sides of the dishes. Bake in the preheated oven for about 1 hour, or until the puddings are set. (To test if set, carefully insert a round bladed knife into the centre; if the knife comes out clean they are set.) Remove the puddings from the roasting tin and allow to cool. Chill in the refrigerator, preferably overnight.

Sprinkle the sugar over the top of each dish and place the puddings under a preheated hot grill. When the sugar has caramelized and turned deep brown, remove from the heat and cool. Chill the puddings in the refrigerator for 2–3 hours before serving.

Toss the raspberries in the remaining caster sugar and sprinkle over the top of each dish. Serve with a little extra cream if liked.

Sauternes Olive Oil Cake

Serves 8–10

125 g/4 oz plain flour, plus extra
for dusting
4 medium eggs
125 g/4 oz caster sugar
grated zest of $^1/_2$ lemon
grated zest of $^1/_2$ orange
2 tbsp Sauternes or other sweet
dessert wine
3 tbsp very best quality
extra-virgin olive oil
4 ripe peaches
1–2 tsp soft brown sugar, or to taste
1 tbsp lemon juice
icing sugar, to dust

Preheat oven to 140°C/ 275°F/Gas Mark 1. Oil and line a 25.5 cm/10 inch springform tin. Sift the flour on to a large sheet of greaseproof paper and reserve. Using a freestanding electric mixer, if possible, whisk the eggs and sugar together, until pale and stiff. Add the lemon and orange zest.

Turn the speed to low and pour the flour from the paper in a slow, steady stream on to the eggs and sugar mixture. Immediately add the wine and olive oil and switch the machine off as the olive oil should not be incorporated completely.

Using a rubber spatula, fold the mixture very gently 3 or 4 times so that the ingredients are just incorporated. Pour the mixture immediately into the prepared tin and bake in the preheated oven for 20–25 minutes, without opening the door for at least 15 minutes. Test if cooked by pressing the top lightly with a clean finger – if it springs back, remove from the oven, if not, bake for a little longer.

Leave the cake to cool in the tin on a wire rack. Remove the cake from the tin when cool enough to handle.

Meanwhile, skin the peaches and cut into segments. Toss with the brown sugar and lemon juice and reserve. When the cake is cold, dust generously with icing sugar, cut into wedges and serve with the peaches.

Churros (Spain)

Serves 4–6

300 ml/¹/₂ pint water
5 tbsp sunflower oil, plus extra
for frying
1 tsp ground cinnamon
finely grated zest of 1 small lemon
200 g/7 oz plain white flour
pinch salt
1 medium egg
oil, for deep-frying
1 tbsp icing sugar, for dusting

Pour the water into a heavy-based saucepan and pour in the oil. Add half the cinnamon with the lemon zest and bring to the boil. Sift the flour with the salt and when the water comes to the boil, tip in the flour and beat well with a wooden spoon over a low heat. Continue to beat until a ball forms in the centre of the pan and the sides are clean of any mixture. Leave to cool for about 5 minutes, then beat in the egg.

When ready to cook, heat the oil for deep-frying in a deep-fat fryer and heat to 180°C/350°F. Have ready a plate lined with absorbent kitchen paper.

Spoon the mixture into a large piping bag fitted with a large nozzle. Only fill the bag to half full, otherwise the mixture will be difficult to pipe.

Once the oil has reached temperature, pipe 7.5 cm/3 inch lengths into the hot oil and cook for 3–4 minutes until golden. Using a slotted spoon, remove the churros carefully from the oil and drain on kitchen paper. Repeat until all the mixture has been used. Dust with the icing sugar mixed with the remaining cinnamon and serve warm.

Sweet-stewed Dried Fruits

Serves 4

500 g/1 lb 2 oz packet mixed
dried fruit salad
450 ml/³/₄ pint apple juice
2 tbsp clear honey
2 tbsp brandy
1 lemon
1 orange

To decorate:

crème fraîche
fine strips pared orange rind

Place the fruits, apple juice, clear honey and brandy in a small saucepan.

Using a small sharp knife or a zester, carefully remove the zest from the lemon and orange and place in the pan. Squeeze the juice from the lemon and orange and add to the pan.

Bring the fruit mixture to the boil and simmer for about 1 minute. Remove the pan from the heat and allow the mixture to cool completely.

Transfer the mixture to a large bowl, cover with clingfilm and chill in the refrigerator overnight to allow the flavours to blend.

Spoon the stewed fruit into 4 shallow dessert dishes. Decorate with a large spoonful of half-fat crème fraîche and a few strips of the pared orange rind and serve.

Baked Stuffed Amaretti Peaches

Serves 4

4 ripe peaches
grated zest and juice
of 1 lemon
8 Amaretti biscuits
50 g/2 oz chopped blanched
almonds, toasted
50 g/2 oz pine nuts, toasted
3 tbsp light muscovado sugar
50 g/2 oz butter
1 medium/large egg yolk
2 tsp clear honey
crème fraîche or Greek yogurt,
to serve

Preheat the oven to 180°C/350°F/Gas Mark 4. Halve the peaches and remove the stones. Take a very thin slice from the bottom of each peach half so that it will sit flat in a baking tray. Dip the peach halves in lemon juice and arrange in the baking tray.

Crush the Amaretti biscuits lightly and put into a large bowl. Add the almonds, pine nuts, sugar, lemon zest and butter. Work with the fingertips until the mixture resembles coarse breadcrumbs. Add the egg yolk and mix well until the mixture is just binding.

Divide the Amaretti and nut mixture between the peach halves, pressing down lightly. Bake in the preheated oven for 15 minutes, or until the peaches are tender and the filling is golden. Remove from the oven and drizzle with the honey.

Place two peach halves on each serving plate and spoon over a little crème fraîche or Greek yogurt, then serve.

Goats' Cheese Lemon Tart

Serves 4

125 g/4¹/₂ oz butter,
cut into small pieces
225 g/8 oz plain flour
pinch salt
50 g/2 oz sugar
1 medium/large egg yolk

For the filling:

350 g/12 oz mild fresh goats' cheese
3 eggs, beaten
150 g/5 oz sugar
grated zest and juice
of 3 lemons
450 ml/³/₄ pint double cream
fresh raspberries, to decorate

Preheat the oven to 200°C/400°F/Gas Mark 6, 15 minutes before cooking. Rub the butter into the plain flour and salt until the mixture resembles breadcrumbs, then stir in the sugar. Beat the egg yolk with 2 tablespoons cold water and add to the mixture. Mix together until a dough is formed, then turn the dough out onto a lightly floured surface and knead until smooth. Chill in the refrigerator for 30 minutes.

Roll the dough out thinly on a lightly floured surface and use to line a 4 cm/1¹/₂ inch deep 23 cm/9 inch fluted flan tin. Chill in the refrigerator for 10 minutes. Line the pastry case with greaseproof paper and baking beans or kitchen foil and bake blind in the preheated oven for 10 minutes. Remove the paper and beans or kitchen foil. Return to the oven for a further 12–15 minutes until cooked. Leave to cool slightly, then reduce the oven temperature to 150°C/300°F/Gas Mark 2.

Beat the goats' cheese until smooth. Whisk in the eggs, sugar, lemon rind and juice. Add the cream and mix well. Carefully pour the cheese mixture into the pastry case and return to the oven. Bake in the oven for 35–40 minutes, or until just set. If the tart begins to brown or swell, open the oven door for 2 minutes, then reduce the temperature to 120°C/250°F/Gas Mark 2 and leave the tart to cool in the oven. Chill in the refrigerator until cold. Decorate and serve with fresh raspberries.

Fig Chocolate Bars

Makes 12

125 g/4 oz butter
50 g/5 oz plain flour
50 g/2 oz soft light
brown sugar
225 g/8 oz ready-to-eat dried
figs, halved
juice of $^1/_2$ a large lemon
1 tsp ground cinnamon
125 g/4 oz dark chocolate

Preheat the oven to 180°C/350°F/Gas Mark 4, 10 minutes before baking. Lightly oil an 18 cm/7 inch square cake tin. Place the butter and the flour in a large bowl and, using your fingertips, rub the butter into the flour until it resembles fine breadcrumbs.

Stir in the sugar, then, using your hand, bring the mixture together to form a smooth dough. Knead until smooth, then press the dough into the prepared tin. Lightly prick the base with a fork and bake in the preheated oven for 20–30 minutes, or until golden. Remove from the oven and leave the shortbread to cool in the tin until completely cold.

Meanwhile, place the dried figs, lemon juice, 125 ml/4 fl oz water and the ground cinnamon in a saucepan and bring to the boil. Cover and simmer for 20 minutes, or until soft, stirring occasionally during cooking. Cool slightly, then puree in a food processor until smooth. Cool, then spread over the cooked shortbread.

Melt the chocolate in a heatproof bowl set over a saucepan of simmering water. Alternatively, melt the chocolate in the microwave, according to the manufacturer's instructions. Stir until smooth, then spread over the top of the fig filling. Leave to become firm, then cut into 12 bars and serve.

Index

Index